Turning Lace Bobbins

By
David Springett

This book is for Robin and Nicola
Whose lives have been dominated by lace and bobbins.

Acknowledgements

I would like to thank the following for the help they gave producing this book.

Mrs. V. M. Beacham - for her proof reading.

John Cummings - for giving me such valuable help when I began turning bobbins.

Janet Dutton - for her bobbin decorating ability.

Ian French - for his help in many ways throughout the book production.

Stuart Johnson - who was always ready to help me find unusual materials.

Lance Riley - the computer whiz.

Christine Springett - always ready to help and encourage me.

First Published 1995 by
C & D Springett

Christine & David Springett
8 Strath Close
Rugby, Warwickshire
CV21 4GA England
Tel. 01788 544691

© David Springett 1995

ISBN 0 - 9517157 4 7

Illustrations © Tim Benké 1995

With the exception of
illustration No.s 4.1, 4.2, 9.1, 9.3, 9.4,
20.7, part 26.1, 35.4. by © Robin Springett 1995

All rights reserved

Printed by Neil Terry Printing, Rugby 568000.

Contents

Introduction

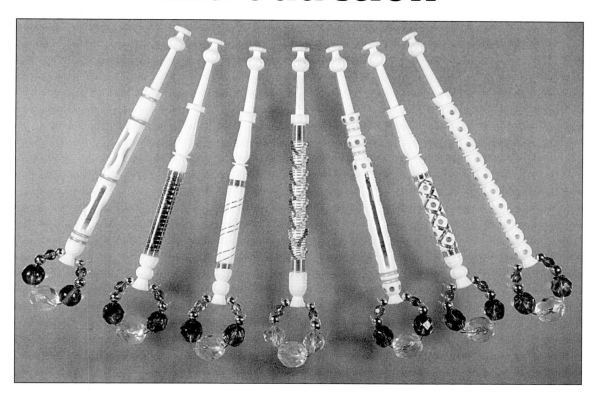

I have been making lace bobbins since 1977 during which time I have learnt a few tricks and developed my own method of turning these lacemaking tools. Almost every bobbinmaker has his or her method of turning but it is the method that I have developed which will be detailed in this book.

The techniques and skills are arranged in a progressive manner from the first chapter onward. Some of the more challenging styles will be found in the bone section but do not feel that they cannot be reproduced in wood or that the styles in the wood section may not be worked in bone. The separation of these styles is purely for convenience.

As there will be some techniques which will be repeated, rather than tediously detailing each step through to the last chapter, as methods of work become familiar their detailed instructions will be dropped.

The main portion of this book will deal with English East Midland lace bobbins for these are the bobbins which have, in the past, developed such a variety of decorative styles. The wide range of lace bobbins made throughout the world today exhibit the most exciting spread of imaginative spindle turning ever seen. Unfortunately it is an unrecognised area of skill in the turning community.

This book cannot hope to cover all the ideas and techniques available. Use your imagination and draw ideas from as wide an area as possible for to be successful as a bobbinmaker a degree of originality is needed. Use this book as a staging post, learn your techniques, develop your skills, look at old bobbins in museums and see how the early craftsmen worked but most of all bring something of your own quality to lace bobbin making.

Finally, it is too easy to slavishly copy that which has gone before. Certainly use styles and designs which you have seen and incorporate them in your own bobbins but it is far more exciting to develop than mimic.

Enjoy turning lace bobbins.

A Brief History

An idealised view of village life.

Lace bobbins have been made as long as lacemakers have needed them. The trade or craft of lace bobbin making has never been an organized occupation, those who made the tools for lacemaking were scattered across the lacemaking counties.

As always excellence prevails and those bobbinmakers with a good reputation sold more bobbins. Early nineteenth century turners such as Jesse and James Compton of Deanshanger, Northamptonshire, William Brown of Cranfield, Bedfordshire, Archibald Abbott of Bedford and Joseph Haskins of Bedford (possibly the best bobbin maker of the nineteenth century) all gained excellent reputations for their skill in producing fine lace bobbins.

Unfortunately even with the large population of lacemakers in Northamptonshire, Bedfordshire, and Buckingham-shire these East Midland bobbinmakers were not always able to support their families using that skill alone, often they became agricultural labourers, or just woodturners and furniture makers. William (bobbin) Brown though, was one of the fortunate few. All his life, on every census on which he was listed, he stated that he was a bobbinmaker.

Looking around a nineteenth century turners workshop all the equipment would be recognisable though the blacksmith made tools might not have the commercial sparkle of those we own today. The treadle lathe, a common but crude sort, would have a tailstock able to be moved back and forth and locked firmly in place using a wedge below. The tailstock centre would be a simple metal point, the chuck, a square hole at the end of the wooden mandrel, much like bobbin chucks available today.

Fig. 0.1 Square block on bobbin end.

I have been most fortunate for when collecting antique bobbins I came upon a bone bobbin which still had the squared block remaining on its end showing that this was exactly how it was held in the lathe. *(Fig. 0.1).*

Treadling away the turner would push the prepared blank into the rotating hole in the mandrel with familiar ease, quickly knocking up the centre to support the end of the work. Once the bobbin had been turned it would be parted off close to the headstock. The waste pip in the bobbin chuck would be knocked out to be replaced with a fresh blank. The whole process quick and efficient, no stopping and starting, just easy production.

The nineteenth century English villages in which these bobbinmakers worked were to a great part self sufficient, with a wide variety of craftsmen and women producing goods to keep the village functioning. Various craftspeople wandered from village to village bringing skills which were only occasionally needed.

The village bobbinmaker (and not all villages had one) would rely upon the various skilled workers to help him maintain his production. For a start the treadle lathe would be the collaborative production of a carpenter (or himself) to make the bed and frame, the wheelwright would make the flywheel and headstock hub, the blacksmith would make any metal parts, and the harnessmaker would be approached for a leather driving belt.

For wood the turner would most probably rely upon the intermittent visits of the pit sawyer who was an itinerant worker with a reputation for drunkenness. The sawyer was often found in the local alehouse at the end of a hard days sawing enthusiastically slaking his thirst. When the pit sawyer arrived in the village his pit, located at the end of the village, would be cleaned out and made ready for work. The various wood using craftsman would bring, for cutting, the logs that they had collected. The bobbinmaker, most probably having gathered an old apple or plum tree from an orchard or a hawthorn toppled out of a hedgerow, would ask for these to be cut into planks. He might choose to have the apple sawn into half-inch thick planks to make allowance for twisting and warping but the hawthorn he would have cut thinner knowing that it is a little more stable. Having paid the sawyer he would haul the planks to his workshop where they would be laid in a covered area with sticks separating each plank. The air could then blow through and around each piece slowly drying the wood over several seasons. The planks when dry would be hand sawn into bobbin blanks.

As most village families would not have been able to afford to eat meat regularly the bobbinmaker would have to travel to one of the larger towns to buy bone from a bone merchant. The bone merchant sold bone as a material or to be ground down into fertiliser. As neither the merchant nor bobbinmaker would be able to tell one type of bone from another the bobbins could well be made from Ox, Beef or Shire horse bone. All bone would have the same working properties. If there was no bone merchant locally then the bobbinmaker might visit the tallow chandler for tallow is produced by boiling down animal bones. The fat is skimmed from the top of the boiling vat and refined into candle tallow or lubricating grease. The remaining bones are then sold and this is where the bobbinmaker has his chance to buy some clean and thick bone.

Bone and wood were the regular materials which the nineteenth century bobbinmaker used. Ivory would be a material they would be unable to afford even if they could find a supplier.

Just because the bobbinmakers of the last century and earlier used what we consider crude equipment don't think that they produced crude work. Some of the finest bobbins I have seen were produced in the nineteenth century. It is the turners skill which counts not his or her equipment.

A selection of turned lace bobbins.

Antique lace bobbins from the 19th Century.

Leopards, Tigers, Butterflies, Bees Knees and many more.

Cow and Calf, Tunbridgeware, Loose Rings, Mother and Babe, and many more.

Tinsel, Inlaid, Double Fairing, Grandmother, Fairing, Arrows and Dyed bobbins.

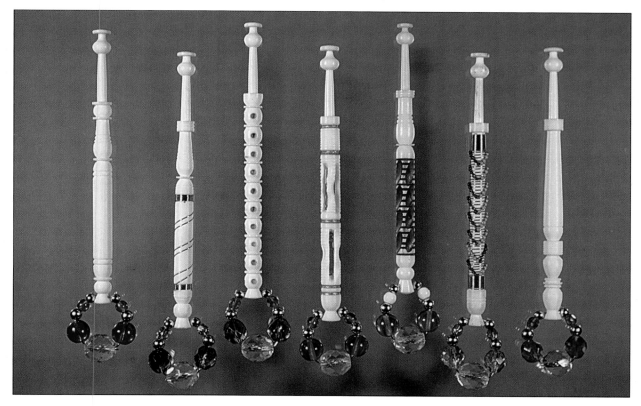

Secret, Candy Wired, Caterpillar, 2D Mother and Babe, Dyed, Chevron Beaded and Decorative bobbins.

Minature lace pillow and bobbins ...

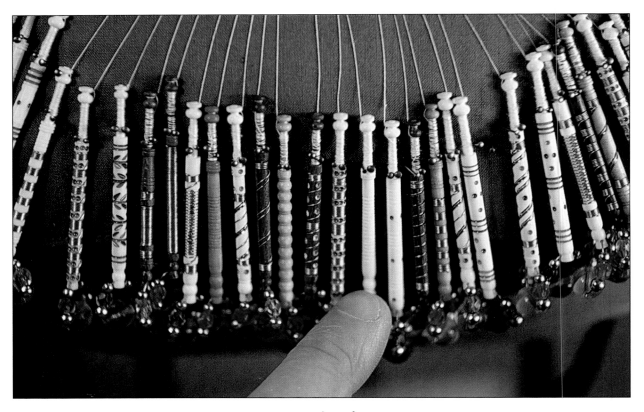

... now in scale.

Part 1

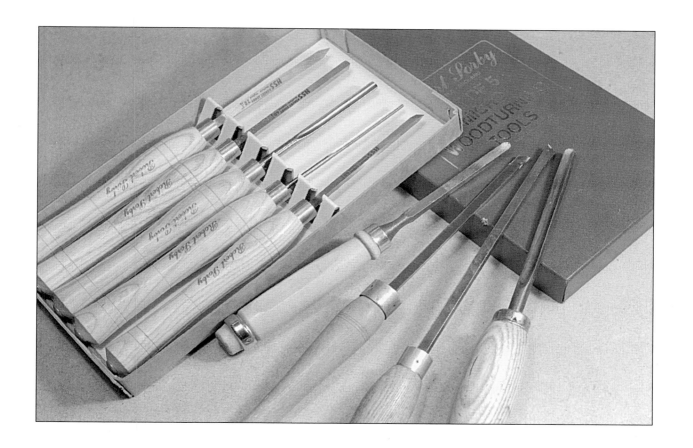

Tools, Materials & Equipment.

1 – Safety

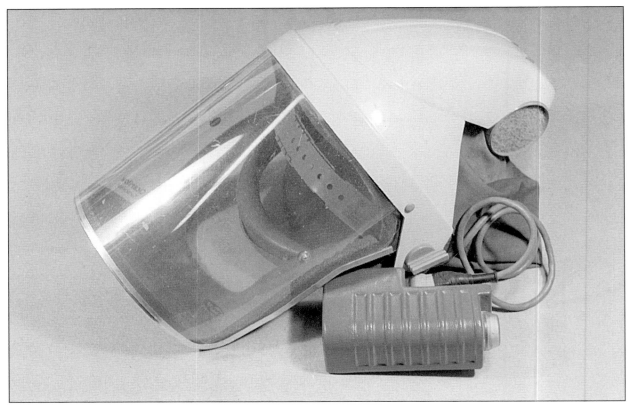

Fig. 1.1 Visor and clean air in one.

When turning lace bobbins all the regular safety rules should be followed.

- As well as protecting your eyes, protect your lungs. I wear a mask which blows clean air across my face, that is ideal, but a small close fitting fabric mask will do for occasional use. (*Fig. 1.1*).

- Always wear goggles or safety glasses.

- Have your work area and the workpiece well lit.

- Make sure all work is fixed firmly in the chuck.

- Be aware of the chuck jaws when turning, do not run the tool or your hands into the rotating chuck.

Care has been taken to present safe methods of work throughout this book The author and publisher cannot be responsible for any accidents or damage caused when working on any of the projects described here.

2 – Materials

One of the many things which makes bobbin making so interesting and challenging is that such a wide variety of materials may be used in their making. It must be remembered that particularly for the head of the bobbin the chosen material must present a smooth surface. Also Woods which bleed colour such as padauk and purpleheart must be well sealed particularly where they make contact with lace thread. (At the head and neck).

Woods

Avoid open grained wood such as Oak and Ash for when turning these small items the "open" parts of the grain can appear as wide gaps which is the last thing that is needed across a delicate lace bobbin head. As bobbins may be turned from joined or laminated parts then many of those relatively small pieces of otherwise unusable or unsuitable fine woods will, at last, have a use.

Other woods which are often overlooked are the backyard exotics such as Mahonia and Berberis. (small shrubs which both produced brilliant yellow wood).

Damson, Plum, and other small fruit trees produced good close grained wood. Lilac, Laburnum, Hawthorn and Privet are all worth trying in fact look around your own or your friends garden and see what wonderful woods have been under your nose for so many years.

If you choose to use wood which you have gathered then cut it or split it lengthways. Seal the endgrain with P.V.A. glue, emulsion paint, wax or polish then leave the pieces outdoors with air space between each piece in an airy but covered area. Allow the pieces of wood to dry naturally before using them.

Of course you must remember that there is available an incredible range of rare and exotic woods from around the world. No matter how expensive they are, because lace bobbins are so small, the unit price makes them affordable, better still search round other turners' scrap boxes for exotic off-cuts.

Bone

Fig. 2.1 Cutting a piece from the bone.

Bone for bobbin making is commercially available. It is far easier to deal with as prepared blanks.

For those who have difficulty buying ready prepared bone then follow the methods detailed below but remember do not use raw bone for it can spread disease.

To obtain bone of sufficient thickness and length it is best to buy, from the butcher, the back leg thigh bone of a beef animal, the older the better. Other bone from sheep or pigs are far too small. Whale bone in some cases may be pithy (full of small holes). Camel bone, Shire horse, Ox, Elephant, and Giraffe bones work well but are not so easily obtained. (I am not suggesting the use of these, just providing information.) Stick to beef bone it works well.

Having bought your big beef bone, first cut the knuckles from either end or arrange for the butcher to do that. Make sure that the longest straight length possible remains. Take a pressure cooker (if not available then the bone will have to be boiled in an open saucepan for two and a half hours) and

fit the bone pieces inside. Cover the bone pieces with water (if the pressure cooker becomes filled to the brim then some bone will have to be removed.). Now a choice, if you want to have soup or stock as well as bone pieces just fit the lid, bring up to pressure and cook for 15 minutes. If you want as much pure white bone as possible (no soup, no stock) then sprinkle one level tablespoonful of washing powder into the water, fit the lid and bring to pressure cooking for 15 minutes. The soap powder helps raise the fat above the bone preventing it from soaking in. Fat soaked bone has small, dull amber coloured, translucent patches.

When fully cooked and the pressure is down carefully remove the lid, skim the fat scum from the surface, remove the bone from the pot and swill under warm water. Leave the bone pieces to dry.

Cutting the bone into pieces.

Now this is quite awkward for although the bone may be thick at either end it may be thinner in the middle, more likely it may have a twist in its length making it difficult to cut a good straight piece. First look at the bone and judge where best to make the first cut. I hold the bone in a workmate and use a hacksaw to cut along its length making the first cut into the hollow centre. Next move the bone around so that a second cut may be made 6mm ($1/4$ inch) away from the first making a wedge shaped piece. *(Fig. 2.2)*.

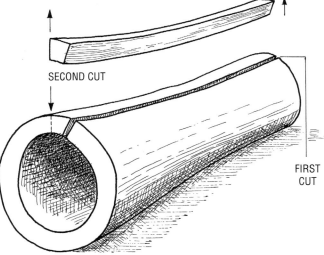

Fig. 2.2 Cutting a piece from the bone.

If you are tempted to cut the bone on a bandsaw then take great care for the irregular shape of the piece can cause problems, in fact I would discourage the use of a bandsaw to cut bone.

From a good bone four to eight pieces may be cut. Badly shaped bones may give only one piece and sometimes none. Don't be discouraged.

Some bone is whiter than others. When in Australia I was always asked what I did to make the bone I used so white. I do nothing other than that described above. The bone I get is white I think it has something to do with the animals diet or maybe it is the breed. Be prepared for off-white bone.

Horn

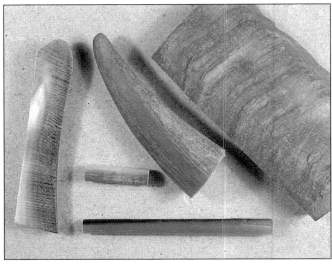

Fig. 2.3 Pieces of ox and buffalo horn.

Oxhorn tips and Buffalo horn may be turned using exactly the same techniques and tools for woodturning but horn does blunt tools rapidly. Some consider the smell from this material to be unpleasant but I feel that the finished product is worth a little discomfort.

When well turned long streams of shavings pour off, occasionally wrapping around the chuck or work. It is best to stop the lathe and clean the shavings away if this happens for it can become difficult to see how the turning is progressing.

Fig. 2.4 Turning ox horn with shavings flying.

If horn becomes too warm when it is being worked it will flex dramatically, so keep the tool and work cool.

Surface finishing

Some horn will have hairline cracks running through, these will not greatly weaken the piece but they will be noticeable, so choose your piece carefully. No matter how carefully you turn horn there will be small areas which appear as slightly rough whitish bruises. To remove these use fine wet and dry abrasive paper and a little Brasso (metal polish), or T-cut, polishing the piece with the lathe running.

Do not try to use what is called "pressed horn" for this is thin sheet horn and will split apart when being turned.

Antler

Antler is worked in exactly the same manner as bone. There are two problems with antler though, it can be a little pithy, and it is very difficult to find pieces thick enough. Two species of deer, the Simbar and the Chittal deer from India produce antlers whose wall thickness is great enough to produce pieces from which to turn bobbins. For all the trouble it is far easier turning bone.

Dymondwood.

An interesting material made from coloured veneers sandwiched together and bonded under pressure with resin. It may be turned like any other piece of wood to produce whole bobbins or used as a central decorative feature in the body of a bobbin.

Crushed Velvet.

Available as pen blanks, this material is a cloudy swirl of coloured resin. It may be turned using the same techniques as those used for turning wood. It works well as a central decorative feature in a lace bobbin rather than using it to turn a whole bobbin.

Fig. 2.5 A variety of materials.

3 – Glues & Polishes.

Glues.

There are three glues I use, P.V.A. for fixing wood parts together, Supaglue (crazy glue / Cyno-acrylate) which repairs hairline cracks or strengthens coarse grain or rough surfaces before they are turned to a finish, and Epoxy Resin for fixing bone parts together.

Polishes.

Most turners have their favourite polish. My favourite for wood bobbins is Speed'n'eze, a friction polish. It is shellac based with some secret ingredient to prevent it from "gripping". For those of you who are unable to buy this type of polish mix French polish with 5% (of volume) linseed oil. This mixture can be applied to the rotating work and polished off with the same cloth. If it doesn't work first time and grips the cloth then add a little more linseed oil to the mixture. This mix is a poor substitute really.

4 – Tools.

Beside those tools normally used for woodturning there are two which are of particular use to bobbinmakers. These are simply made from cheap imported wood chisels.

The first is a square end tool made from a 6mm (^{1}/$_4$ inch) wood chisel. It is turned on its edge showing a 3mm (^{1}/$_8$ inch) thickness and ground back at about 80 degrees leaving a square front edge. The edges are relief ground to prevent the tool from gripping. *(Fig. 4.1).*

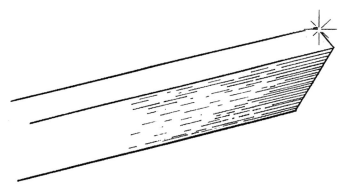

Fig. 4.1 Square end tool ground to about 80 degrees.

The second is a round nose tool, again made from the same size chisel but this time the wide flat surface faces up and the cutting edge is ground to a semicircle. Grind back at about 80 degrees *(Fig. 4.2).*

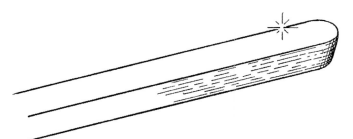

Fig. 4.2 Round nose tool ground to about 80 degrees.

A skew chisel is a regular turning tool. The one I use is slightly different. Made from a length of 6mm (^{1}/$_4$ inch) square tool steel, two faces are ground across the diagonal ends of that bar to come to a cutting edge with an included angle of around 45 degrees. *(Fig. 4.3).* I have found this skew particularly easy to use but if you have a favourite of your own then stick with that. For a supply of square steel for this tool see "Useful Addresses."

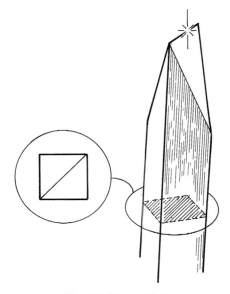

Fig. 4.3 Skew chisel.

Remember when using a grindstone to wear eye protection and have a bowl of water ready to cool the tool.

For miniature turning I do use two smaller tools; a skew similar to that described but made from 3mm (^{1}/$_8$ inch) square tool steel and a square end tool 2mm (^{1}/$_{12}$ inch) wide and 4mm (^{1}/$_6$ inch) deep, again made from tool steel.

Of course there are many excellent tools on the market so if you don't want to make your own look around and you could easily buy them.

If when grinding tools from these cheap wood chisels the tool is overheated and it loses its temper do not be too concerned for hardening and tempering is a simple process.

Hardening And Tempering.

Fig. 4.4 Heating the tool in a gas flame.

Using a gas torch heat the tool to bright red heat *(Fig. 4.4)* and then immediately quench in a salt water solution (about 2 tablespoons of salt to 1 pint of water). This solution does not cool the tool as aggressively as tap water. Move the tool moderately slowly around in the water to cool, a fast movement will not speed the cooling.

Clean the surface of the now cool tool using an abrasive paper. Place the shiny tool once more into the gas flame so that the central portion of the tool is gently heated. Move the tool in and out of the flame so that the temperature of the tool is raised slowly. Watch the bright metal and oxide colours will appear, first pale straw, then brown moving to purple, then blue and onward. If the tool is heated gently then these coloured oxide bands will be wide and that is exactly what is required.

Encourage these coloured bands towards the tip of the tool by stroking the flame along the tool length. A broad band of blue exactly at the tip of the tool is needed, so watch the colours as they move towards the tip and immediately blue touches the end quench it in the salt water.

These oxide bands are a guide to the crystalline structure of the metal beneath. Quenching at blue will give the required hardness to the cutting edge.

This blue area will eventually be sharpened away but don't worry, for the hardening and tempering process may be repeated.

5 – Equipment.

The Pendant Drill.

This consists of a motor, suspended above the lathe, with a flexible drive shaft having a collet chuck at its end. This chuck accepts small drills, burrs and grindstones. It has a foot control which can increase and decrease the speed leaving the hands free to manipulate the rotating tool.

Most of the tasks the pendant drill performs can be carried out using files and other hand tools but it is far quicker and simpler to use this electrically driven tool.

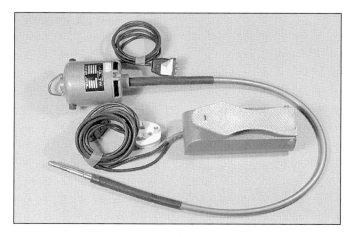

Fig. 5.1 Pendant drill and foot pedal as purchased.

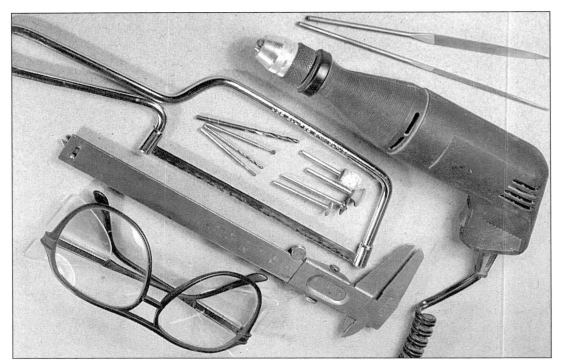

Fig. 5.2 Dremel tool, junior hacksaw, burrs, vernier gauge, needle files and safety glasses

Dremel Tool.

The dremel tool is a small hand held drill with a chuck which will hold small drills, burrs, and grindstones. Once this tool is switched on it remains at full speed until switched off.

Junior Hacksaw.

A very useful tool but remember; always buy the best quality blades, cheap blades bend, break and wear quickly.

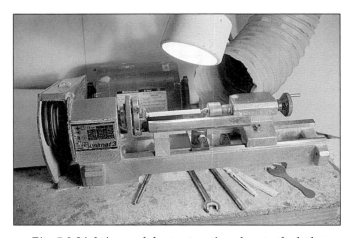

Fig. 5.3 Lighting and dust extraction close to the lathe.

Needlefiles.

Have a selection of needlefiles available for they are always useful for cleaning out awkward areas.

Burrs, Drills, & Grindstones.

Once you have an understanding of the cuts or the shaping you wish to do then look at the variety of burrs, drills, and grindstones that are available at your hardware store. Dremel have an excellent range. You may wish to ask your Dentist to show you the various dental burrs he or she uses. If you are on good terms with the Dentist you may be able to buy some burrs from him (or her).

Lighting & Dust Extraction.

Although these may not be considered to be pieces of equipment necessary in the production of lace bobbins I think that they are very important.

Make sure that the lathe and the piece which is being turned is well lit. There are many neat light fittings available so go get one.

More and more I feel that removing dust at source is most important so if you can afford it buy a dust extractor.

6 – The Lathe.

I use a Unimat 3 lathe made by Emco. It is small which means I can get closer to the work and not be encumbered by a large headstock. This lathe also has a hollow mandrel and an excellent three jaw chuck enabling small diameter pieces to be pushed well inside the headstock.

I have exchanged the small motor which was fitted to this lathe for a $^1/_4$ horsepower motor from an old washing machine. Running at about 1,250. R.P.M. the speed can be stepped up using a pulley to drive the lathe at 1,750 R.P.M.. For these smaller diameter pieces this high speed is essential.

There are several other good small lathes available. Carbatech, and Bonnie Klein both produce small lathes, but it is best to look around and ask advice from those who have such lathes before making your final decision.

If you have a larger lathe and do not wish to buy a small lathe just for bobbinmaking use a drill chuck and fit that to your headstock. A bobbin chuck may be useful for holding squares to be rounded down. Those with a hollow mandrel will find a Jacobs chuck, with a Morse taper to match the mandrel, ideal. Those with a solid mandrel

need to look carefully at the large range of chucks on offer, it would be best to find a small smooth edged chuck rather than a three or four jaw chuck for the rapidly rotating jaws could be dangerous for an inexperienced bobbin turner. It is best if the chuck that is chosen enables at least 50mm. (2 inches) of the bobbin blank to be held inside.

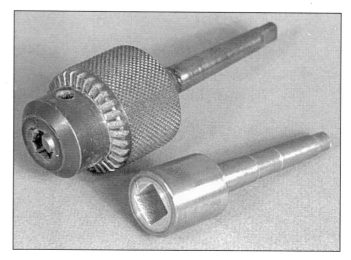

Fig. 6.2 Jacobs chuck and bobbin chuck.

No matter which lathe and chuck is used be particularly careful of chuck jaws. When the lathe is switched on the jaws become a blur. The whirring ghost images of the jaws look harmless and they are unless your knuckles hit them.

Fig. 6.1 The unimat lathe looking well used.

The chuck can be used as an index to assist in the division of the bobbin into sections, thirds, quarters or a mixture of the two. If the chuck has jaws then paint a dot on one jaw so that it may be used as a datum. If a collet chuck is used and the outside is smooth then paint a dot at one point on the outside and again this may be used as a datum point.

When dividing the bobbin into four consider the chuck as a clockface. Begin with the datum at 12 o' clock, mark along the bobbin, now move the datum to 3 o'clock, mark along the bobbin, move the datum jaw to 6 o'clock, mark the bobbin again, then finally move the datum jaw to 9 o'clock and mark the bobbin for the last time.

If it is necessary to divide the bobbin into three equal parts then set the datum jaw first to 12 o'clock, then 4 o'clock, and 8 o'clock marking at each of these positions.

You may consider marking the four dividing points with a white dot of paint and the three dividing points with a red dot of paint. Use the white dots as an index to divide the bobbin into four and the red dots as an index to divide the bobbin into three.

7 – The Lace Bobbin.

It's Design And Function.

A lace bobbin is a tool and it must function perfectly to be acceptable. Once its function is fulfilled the rest of the shaping and decoration can be as wild and exciting as the imagination of the turner.

The body of the bobbin is a handle. It is the area where it is picked up keeping any dirt or grease away from the thread. *(Fig.7.1).*

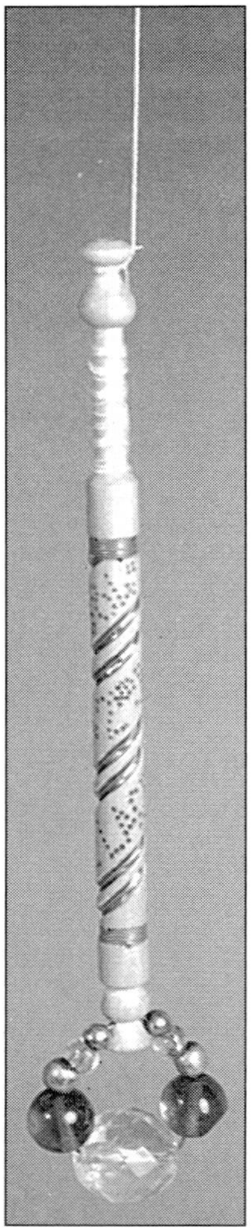

Fig. 7.2 Bobbin on a thread.

The thread is wrapped around the long neck. As some lace patterns require a considerable amount of thread the length and diameter of this part must be of a suitable size to accept sufficient thread.

● The Head.

On East midland bobbins there is a double head. The thread which is wound around the neck comes up and onto the double head to be fixed around the short neck using a double hitch. This prevents the thread unwinding unexpectedly but also allows controlled unwinding. *(Fig. 7.2).*

On other bobbins such as the Devon style, which has a single pancake head, then the double hitch is made just below the head.

*It is important that the top of the head, the part where the single thread leaves the bobbin for good, should have no sharp edges for sharp edges can easily cut the thread.

The thread may be re-wound onto the neck or un-wound as required, the double hitch allows the bobbin to hang at the pillow. It is most important that the head design allows this to happen, for heads which will not hold thread, causing the bobbin to slip from the pillow unravelling the thread, are all but useless.

● The Spangle

The spangle, the ring of beads at the tail of East midland bobbins, adds weight and prevents the bobbin from rolling and twisting.

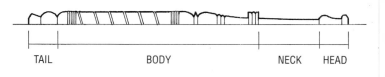

TAIL   BODY   NECK   HEAD

Fig. 7.1 The lace bobbin.

8 – My Method of Production.

My method of turning has been developed for production, speed and efficiency and is based upon preparation of stock. The blanks I produce, heads and necks turned with a plain body, have several advantages.

The first is that by turning heads and necks in quantity the repetition produces uniformity and stock blanks are rapidly produced.

The second advantage is that any form of decoration can be speedily worked upon the plain body of the bobbin giving enormous flexibility to bobbin production.

The third and most useful advantage is that the normally thin and whippy bobbin is turned in two parts. The head and neck first, the short length of the thin neck helps prevent flexing of the workpiece. The head and neck are then firmly supported in a simple collet which is held in the chuck. Again only a short length of work is exposed when turning the body which reduces flexing.

Making The Collets

These simple collets are made in brass. Depending upon the size of the hole drilled through their centre before they are cut in half they can hold various sizes of bobbin neck. (Fig.8.1).

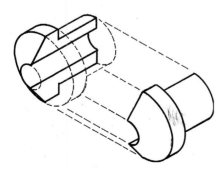

Fig. 8.1 A pair of collets.

Look for useful pieces of brass around 9mm ($^3/_8$ inch) diameter. Maybe an old brass bolt or heavy screw. I have been told that in the plumbing department of the B&Q store brass manifold plugs are available and are ideal.

Take a piece of 9mm ($^3/_8$ inch) brass and hold it in the chuck of your woodturning lathe. Leave about 15mm ($^5/_8$ inch) exposed from the chuck. Take the square ended tool and face off the end of the brass as carefully as you would a piece of wood but finer cuts are needed.

Fig. 8.2 Drilling into the brass.

Select a drill which is the same size as the turned neck of your bobbin, (I usually turn necks around 3mm [$^1/_8$ inch] diameter.) Fit the drill into a drill chuck and fix it to the tailstock. Drill into the brass to a depth of just over 10mm ($^5/_{12}$ inch), withdraw the drill and pull back the tailstock. *(Fig. 8.2).*

Using the round nose tool chamfer the exposed end of the brass - about 2mm ($^1/_{12}$ inch) wide and deep. *(Fig. 8.3).*

Measure a further 2mm ($^1/_{12}$ inch) from the chamfer edge and mark in pencil. From that point

Fig. 8.3 Chamfering the end of the brass piece.

measure 6mm ($^1/_4$ inch) towards the chuck. Using a square end tool turn this section down to 7.5mm ($^5/_{16}$ inch) diameter *(Fig. 8.4)*.

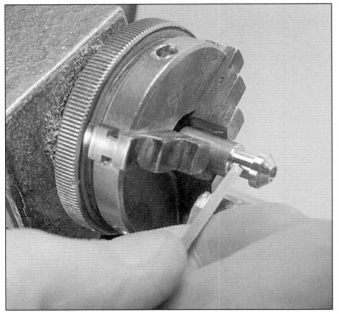

Fig. 8.4 Turning into the body of the brass.

Use the corner of the square end tool at the marked point close to the chuck to cut into the brass. Then sweep along moving towards the right stopping at the marked position 4mm ($^1/_6$ inch) from the face. Continue these light cuts until the required diameter is achieved.

When all the shaping is complete switch off the lathe. Using a hacksaw cut off the 10mm ($^5/_{12}$ inch) turned length of brass. *(Fig. 8.5)*.

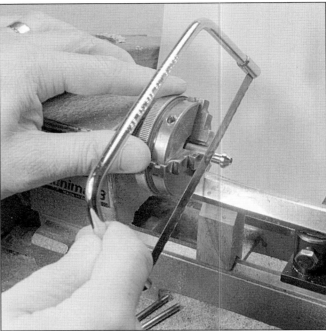

Fig. 8.5 Sawing off the brass bit.

Take the turned collet and hold it in a vice with the drill hole vertical. Using a junior hacksaw carefully cut down through the hole slicing the brass into two matching parts. *(Fig.8.6 & 8.7)*.

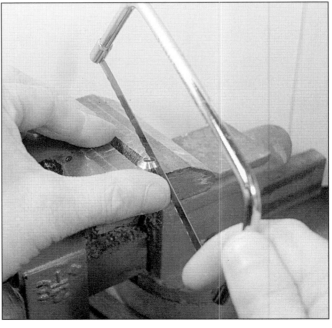

Fig.8.6 Cutting the collet into two parts.

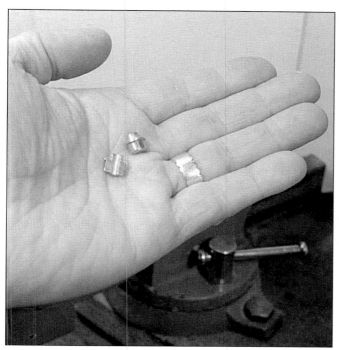

Fig. 8.7 The two halves of the collet.

Carefully file the sawn faces of each collet half.

If you decide to make other collets with larger or smaller holes then an identification mark on each half will help match the pairs.

Re-sharpen your tools before turning.

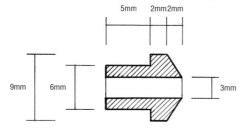

Fig. 8.8 Sizes for the collet.

9 – Making Wood Dowel.

I buy most of my wood for bobbin turning as dowel. Now I know many other turners are not so fortunate in finding a supplier of exotic wood dowel so here is a description of a simple dowel maker loosely based upon a production model.

The Principle.

A length of square section wood is rotated and passed by the edge of a speeding router bit (in this case a 12mm [$1/2$ inch] diameter two flute bit.) As the square section wood rotates next to the cutter the corners are trimmed producing a round section. The forward movement produces a continuous length of dowel. *(Fig. 9.1).*

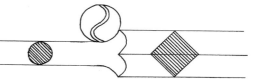

Fig. 9.1 The rotating router bit trims the square into round.

The dimensions for this dowel maker will be specific to the router I use, the bit held and the production of 6mm ($1/4$ inch) dowel. The principle is basic and if understood then different types of router and router bits may be used to produce various sizes of dowel. *(fig. 9.2).*

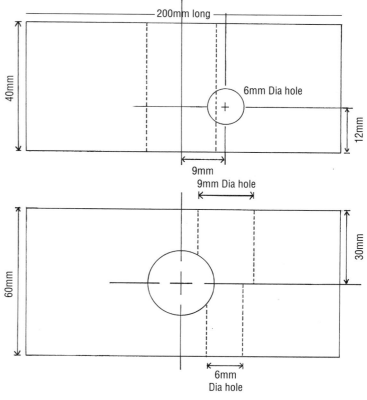

Fig. 9.2 Dimensions for the dowel maker.

The Device.

A block of wood is fixed to the router base with a hole drilled through to allow free movement of the rotating router bit. A second hole, the size of the dowel to be produced, is drilled at right angles and at a tangent to the outside curve that the rotating bit creates. This drilled dowel hole is counter-bored to accept the square section wood allowing it to pass by the router to be trimmed round. *(Fig. 9.3.)*.

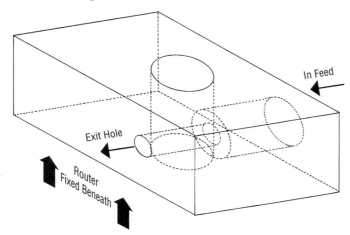

Fig. 9.3 The block and holes drilled through.

Some Points To Consider.

1. The counter-bored hole size equals the measurement across the diagonal of the square section blank -in this case rather conveniently 9mm ($^3/_8$ inches).

2. The dowel blank may be rotated using a brace but this produces a spiral along the dowel. (No real problem if the dowel is to the turned.) If clean smooth dowel is needed then fit the end of the blank into an electric drill and when it is rotating at speed feed it reasonably slowly across the router bit.

3. The hole around the router bit allows wood chips to fall away so add about 6mm ($^1/_4$ inch) to the bit size to arrive at that hole diameter.

4. The distance that the centre of the dowel hole is set away from the centre of the router bit is simply calculated as follows. *(Fig.9.4.)*. Half the diameter of the router bit plus half the diameter of the dowel hole. (In this case that will be half of 12mm [$^1/_2$ inch] plus half 6mm [$^1/_4$ inch] which equals 9mm [$^3/_8$ inch.])

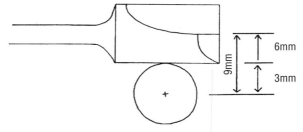

Fig. 9.4 The router bit and dowel.

5. The exit dowel hole may be counter-bored (not all the way) to make it easier for the finished dowel to move through.

6. When first testing this dowel maker the dowel cut at the start of the blank may be a little too large to fit the drilled exit hole. (Of course it may also be a perfect fit first time.) If the dowel produced is too large switch the router off and unplug, then use a round file to widen the exit hole taking care not to strike the router bit. Try making the dowel again. If after several attempts there is still no success choose a drill 0.5mm ($^1/_{32}$ inch) larger than that used for the exit hole and drill it out. *(Fig.9.5)*.

7. The exit hole may need lubricating with paraffin wax occasionally.

8. Wear safety glasses when cutting the dowel.

9. Keep fingers away from the rotating bit.

Fig. 9.5 The dowel maker in use.

Part 2
Wooden Bobbins

10 -- Heads & Necks in Wood.

Having cut the dowel to length, 95mm (3 $^3/_4$ inch), hold the piece in the chuck with about 40mm (1 $^5/_8$ inch) exposed.

Bring the tailstock centre up to support the dowel end. Using your judgment centre the point in the end of the dowel. If the dowel runs on centre fine, if not make adjustments until it does.

Use the gouge to turn the outer surface smooth removing as little wood as possible.

Take the head and neck template and transfer the marks to the dowel using a pencil. The head end of the template is lined up with the end of the dowel at the tailstock end. *(Fig.10.1).*

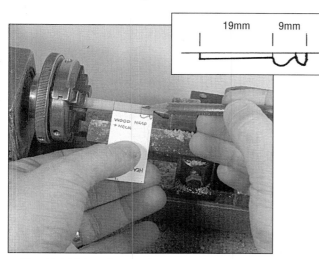

Fig. 10.1 Using the template to mark out the head and neck.

Using a square end tool cut into the neck at the shoulder end (furthest from the head). Move the square end tool slightly from side to side whilst cutting, this will widen the groove sufficiently to prevent the sides of the tool being grabbed by the rotating work. The neck should be turned down close to 3mm ($^1/_8$ inch) diameter at this point. *(Fig.10.2).*

Fig. 10.2 The square end tool cutting at the marked position.

Next use the gouge to rough out, from the head to the shoulder, turning down close to 3mm ($^1/_8$ inch). *(Fig 10.3).*

Fig. 10.3 Roughing down from head to shoulder.

Use the skew first to shape the top of the head down towards the revolving centre. Next work on the small neck area and begin to form the top part of the head. *(Fig. 10.4).*

Fig. 10.4 Shaping the small neck with the skew.

Now move to the bulb working from that position down and in with a sweeping cut into the small neck to meet the previous cut. Once the small neck and part of the bulb has been shaped work the bulb over fluently to meet the neck. Make sure that the bulb is a smooth onion shape. *(Fig. 10.5).*

Fig. 10.5 The bulb of the head being shaped.

Finally use the square end tool to finish the neck clean, straight and smooth. If the square end tool is twisted anti-clockwise slightly and moved from right to left, then twisted clockwise and moved from left to right it will be found that it will act as a small skew slicing shavings from the neck. This simple technique may require a little practice. *(Fig. 10.6).*

Fig. 10.6 Cleaning up the neck.

Clean up the corners close to the head and the shoulder close to the body using the corner of the square end tool.

Fig. 10.7 The finished head.

11 – Some Points To Consider.

This is delicate work and a light touch is required. It may take a little while to reach the point of understanding exactly how much weight to give to the tool. Do not be dismayed if several breakages occur. Please persevere for it does become easier.

It is important that the head is perfectly smooth for any dents, dimples or cracks will catch thread making the bobbin difficult to use. Try to ensure that the clean crisp finish comes from the tools for although I glass-paper the finished head it is only a light touch to remove whiskers. Too heavy a use of glass-paper will remove all the delicacy of the turning.

The bobbin is a tool and the head shape is the most important part of that tool. It should hold the thread firmly whilst working, yet allow it to slip through the hitch when the thread needs to the unwound. Try to develop a head shape which you like BUT please make sure that it works well. I'm sure that you will be able to find plenty of eager lacemakers to test your bobbins and they will certainly let you know how good or bad they are.

Remember that which raises a fair bobbin to an excellent bobbin is often the crispness of the turning. Avoid excessive glass-papering for this causes finished work to look as though it has been squeezed rather than turned.

12 – Beginning to turn East Midland Bobbins.

As many of the body shapes will be quite similar if not exactly in form then in production it seems unnecessary to continually repeat that basic method of turning. Here I will explain how the basic body is turned with grooves for wire if needed, shaping the tail, turning the collar close to the head and the smaller more delicate collar closer to the central decorated area. Pick and choose how these features are applied to the bobbin shape, then decorated appropriately.

Hold the head and neck of the bobbin blank, using collets, in the chuck. Bring the revolving centre forward to support the tail making sure it runs as close to centre as possible. (Fig. 12.1).

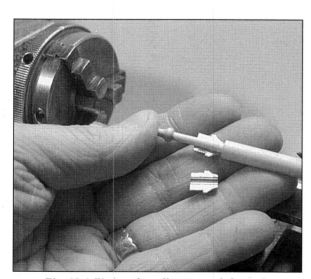

Fig. 12.1 Fitting the collets around the neck.

Using a 9mm ($^3/_8$ inch) gouge skim the surface of the blank so that it is true and even.

Take the chosen template and mark in pencil the major points of the bobbin on the rotating blank stock

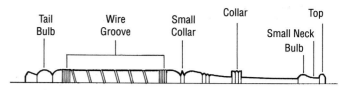

Fig. 12.2. Bobbin part names.

● Turning The Tail. (Fig. 12.3).

Take the square end tool and using slicing cuts shape the angled tail.

Fig. 12.3. Turning the tail.

● Wire Grooves & Collar Preparation.

To work more efficiently if there are wire grooves it is best to cut them whilst the square end tool is being used. At the marked positions use the square end tool as you would a parting tool cutting to a depth of about 1mm ($^1/_{24}$ inch) or the thickness of the wire to be used. At the collar close to the head again cut a groove to a depth of about 1.5mm ($^1/_{16}$ inch). When using the square end tool in this manner move it from side to side very slightly this will prevent the edges from gripping and being drawn in. (Fig. 12.4).

● Shaping The Tail, Bead, Mid - Collar & Main Collar.

Place the square end tool down and take the skew chisel to slice the end of the tail towards the revolving centre.

Fig. 12.4. Cutting wire grooves.

Next shape the bead close to the tail. Use a rolling slicing cut moving towards the right from the top down to the tail. Several cuts will need to be made. (Fig. 12.5).

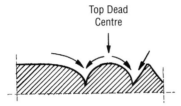

Top Dead
Centre

Fig. 12.5. How the bulb and tail are shaped.

Now for the left side of the bead. From the top of the bead take a slicing cut rolling over down to the left side this time the cut will be made into the body of the bobbin not into a space as on the tail side so a similar cut needs to be made from the body side to create a hollow. — So one rolling slicing cut from the top of the bead to the left followed by a similar cut from the body down to the right meeting to form a valley. This shapes

Fig. 12.6. Turning the bulb.

the bead and the rounded end of the body. (Fig. 12.6). When satisfied move on to the mid - collar. Take the skew and firmly mark, using the point, a line at the pencil mark. Make the same rolling slicing cut from the body into that mark producing a rounded shoulder. Slice down into the pencil marked area to cut a crisp edge to form one side of the collar.

With the skew firmly mark, using the point, a line a little to the left of the pencil mark this will define the width of this thin collar. Repeat the rolling slicing cut down into the marked position producing a curved shoulder on the left of the thin collar. It may be necessary to slice down the edge of the collar to produce a crisp edge. (Fig.12.7).

Fig. 12.7. The curved shoulder to the small collar is turned.

● *The Main collar.*

If the Main collar is shaped with a bead between two uprights like a tomato between two pieces of bread, use the skew in the same manner for turning the bead close to the tail. This time make sure that the cut either side of the bead is more upright keeping the "bread" thick sliced. On the body side of the "slice of bread" use the square end tool to cut a groove about 1.5mm ($^1/_{16}$ inch) deep. Use the gouge to make a sweeping cut from the mid collar bulb towards the head into the turned groove. The skew chisel can be used to make the finishing cut.

Any decorative grooves can be run in using the corner of the square end tool.

13 – Bees Knees.
(Made in Dymondwood.)

I f a bee's leg is viewed through a magnifying glass it appears to be made up of a series of steps or "knees". It is suggested that this traditional bobbin's resemblance to the bee's leg or "knee" gave it its name. *(Fig. 13.4).*

● Hold the blank by its head and neck in collets in the chuck.

● Support the tail end with a revolving centre making sure that it is held on centre.

● Using the gouge skim the blank to a regular and clean 6mm ($^1/_4$ inch) diameter.

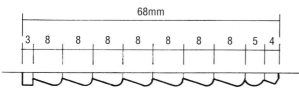

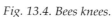

Fig. 13.1. Template.

● Take the template and transfer the major points, in pencil, to the rotating blank. *(Fig.13.1&13.2).*

● Using the square end tool take slicing cuts to shape the angled tail. *(Fig. 13.3).*

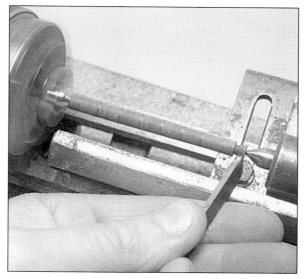

Fig. 13.3. Turning the tail.

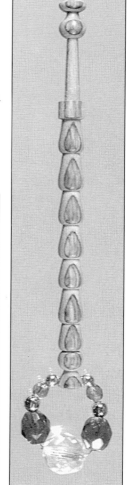

Fig. 13.4. Bees knees.

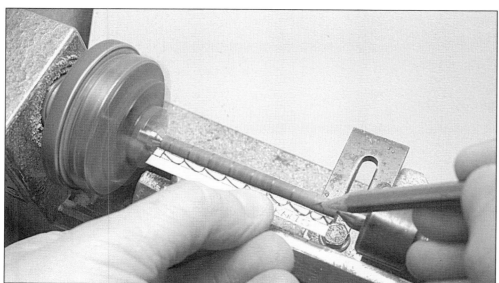

Fig. 13.2. Transferring details from the template.

Fig. 13.5. Rounding over the first "knee".

- Angle down from the first knee towards the second knee using series slicing cuts. Make sure that this angled cut and the top of the knee blend fluently. *(Fig.13.7).*

- Round over second knee. Use the point of the skew to make the initial mark at the start of the third knee. Angle down from the second knee towards the third knee blending the shape and continue down the body turning the series of knees.

- Once all the knees are cleanly cut use fine glass-paper and lightly clean off but do not soften the edges.

- Switch off the lathe, apply the friction polish, then with the lathe running polish to a high gloss.

- Place the square end tool down and take the skew chisel to shape the remaining parts of this bobbin.

- Clean off the end of the tail towards the revolving centre.

- Shape the tailstock side of the bead using a rolling, slicing cut.

- Mark the headstock side of the bead using the point of the skew then make a series of rolling, slicing cuts to produce a fully rounded bead.

- Round over the top of the first knee into the hollow next to the shaped bead. *(Fig.13.5).*

- Using the point of the skew make the initial mark at the start of the second knee. *(Fig.13.6).*

Fig. 13.7. Cutting down from the knee.

Don't "fiddle" when making the series of cuts down the body of the bee's knees; make sure that all cuts are positive and direct. Hesitant cuts will cause the bobbin to lose its fluency.

Fig. 13.6. Marking the start of the second knee.

14 – Spiral Wire & Spot.
(Made In Ebony).

The spiral wire and spot form of decoration is as old as bobbins. It is such a simple and straightforward style yet very effective. Change the colour of the spots, make them larger or smaller, mix the sizes or change the layout of the dots and there is such a variety produced from such a simple idea.

The wood chosen here is Ebony and it is ideal for it provides a plain background for the coloured dots. More importantly it is very dense which prevents the paint from running into the grain and staining around the drilled dot. If you cannot find a piece of Ebony choose any other plain dense wood.

● Turn the head and neck, hold it in collets in the chuck. Bring the tailstock, holding the centre, forward to support the end of the blank. Use a small gouge to skim the surface of the blank so that it is true and even.

● Using the template transfer the main points to the revolving blank using a pencil. *(Fig.14.1).*

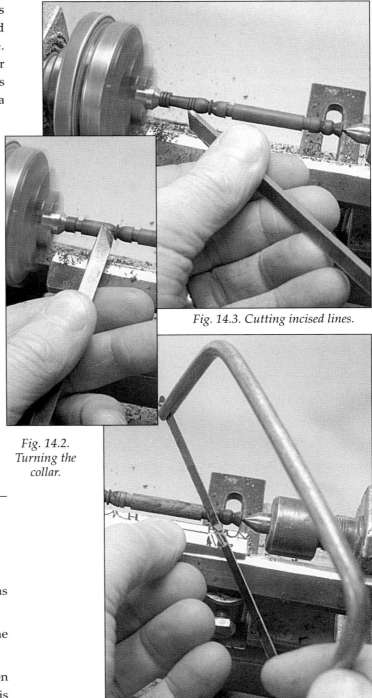

Fig. 14.3. Cutting incised lines.

Fig. 14.2.
Turning the
collar.

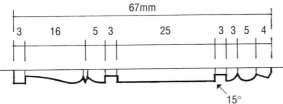

Fig. 14.1. Template.

● Turn the tail, wire grooves, collar and shape as described earlier. *(Fig.14.2&14.3).*

● When the body has been turned to shape, the spiral wire groove can be cut.

● Take a junior hacksaw. Remove the blade then replace it so that the teeth cut backwards. This prevents the blade from cutting so aggressively.

● Set the saw in the wire groove close to the tailstock at 15 degrees to the bobbin. This angle can be marked on the template which can then be used

Fig. 14.4. The saw set to 15 degrees.

as a guide for setting the saw correctly. If a tighter or looser spiral is required then alter the angle accordingly. *(Fig. 14.4).*

● Hold the saw in right hand. (left handers, who no doubt have become used to right handed methods, will have to use this technique for it is very difficult to hold the saw in the left hand and turn the chuck with the right.) Place the left hand on the chuck. Move the saw lightly backwards and forwards at the set angle and at the same time with the left hand rotate the chuck slowly anti-clockwise. A regular spiral saw cut will be made. It may be sensible, if you are unsure of this simple technique, to practice on some less valuable piece of wood until the method is mastered. Once the rotation and the angled cut are coordinated it will be very easy to cut any desired angle. *(Fig. 14.5).*

Fig. 14.6. White pencil marks on the bobbin.

● Move the index jaw to 3 o'clock and mark a line in pencil across the top of the bobbin from one groove to the next.

● Move the chosen index jaw to 6 o'clock and mark the third line in pencil across the top of the bobbin from one wire groove to the other.

● Finally move the index jaw to 9 o'clock and mark a pencil line across the top of the bobbin, wire groove to wire groove.

● The bobbin has been quartered down its length.

● Take each line and between each turn of the spiral groove mark the centre point, the position for the drilled dot.

● Select a round ended burr and fit it into a dremel tool or flexible drive shaft. *(Fig. 14.7).*

Fig. 14.5. Cutting the spiral.

Marking The Position Of The Spots.

● Use one of the jaws as an index.

● Bring the chosen jaw to 12 o'clock.

● Using a pencil, mark a line across the top of the bobbin body from one wire groove to the other. This will run across the cut spiral groove. *(Fig. 14.6).*

With dark woods like Ebony, pencil lines may not show up clearly so buy a white pencil crayon and use that for marking out.

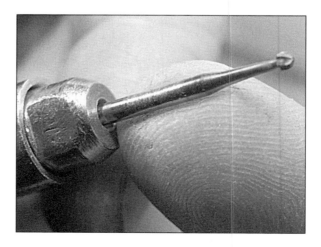

Fig. 14.7. A round burr.

- Hold the rotating burr vertically above the marked position on the pencil line between the cut grooves. Push the burr down into the bobbin at that point cutting a small hemispherical hollow. Repeat this operation at each of the marked points between the cut grooves on each of the four marked lines. *(Fig. 14.8)*.

Fig. 14.8. Drilling the dots.

- When all the holes have been drilled lightly glass-paper the bobbin (don't rub out sharp edges) then polish.

- Leave the bobbin in the lathe so that the dots may be coloured.

- Before colour is applied take the round burr out of the flexible drive and use it to clean out each of the dots, twisting it between the fingers. This ensures that it does not remove any more wood but does clean out excess polish from the hole.

- Humbrol enamel paint is ideal for colouring the dots. Make sure the paint is well stirred or shaken then simply apply the paint into the hollow using a dressmaker's pin.

Fig. 14.9. Painting the dots.

- Take a pin, push it point first into a piece of dowel (or turn a handle) then using wire cutters clip off the pin head.

- Dip this blunt end into the paint, not too deeply. It will pick up sufficient to transfer to the dot and the paint will run down and fill the dot. Make sure it comes to the rim, if necessary encourage it by moving the pin. Use as many colours that you decide will look good. Now leave the paint to dry. *(Fig. 14.9)*.

> *If any colour has run over the hole rim pick up less paint next time. This time just quickly rub your finger over to remove the excess. Wipe your finger on a piece of cloth and repeat until the bobbin is clean.*

- When the bobbin is fully dry take a 1mm ($1/24$ inch) drill and drill the tail. Next drill into the tail end of the wire groove at the edge closest to the tail. Drill into the wire groove at the head end at the edge closest to the head. These drilled holes are to take the wire when winding it onto the bobbin. The method of winding the wire into the spiral groove will be dealt with in the chapter headed "Decorating Bobbins."

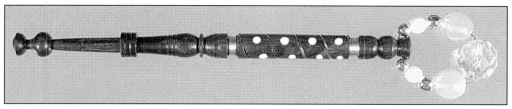

Fig. 14.10. The spiral wire and spot.

15 – Fairing (Made In Boxwood).

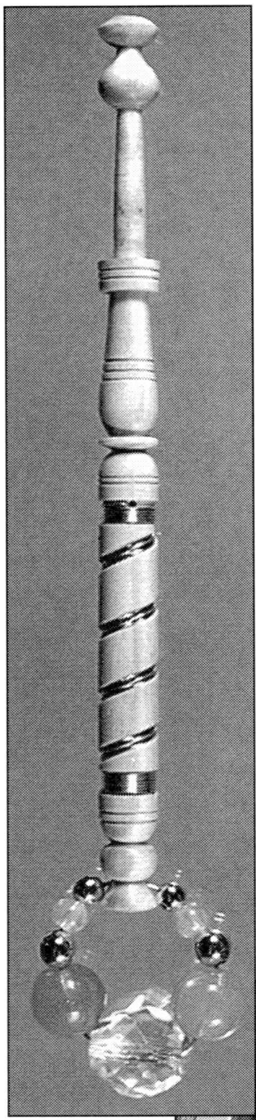

During the last century at hiring fairs, goose fairs, in fact any general fair around the country many bright, shiny highly coloured pieces were sold. Glittering china ornaments, fancy baubles, cheap sparkling jewellery, were all made to attract the unsophisticated country boy or girl. These dazzling geegaws became known as fairings and so eventually any object with glitter and sparkle held that name. It is no surprise then that brightly tinsel decorated bobbins became known as fairings even though many may not have been purchased at a fair.

In the 1800's the tinsel which was used to decorate these bobbins was made from thin sheets of coloured tin. Narrow strips of this "tinsel" were wrapped around the bobbin and held in place with brass wire. A spiral groove was hand filed with a flat bottom to take the metal strip. Today I use modern coloured plastic foil as decoration and I cut the spiral grooves simply by hand completing the cut using a rotary burr.

I have turned the blank with a head and a neck from Boxwood which will show the coloured tinsel to good effect. *(fig. 15.1).*

- Hold the head and neck in the headstock using the collets. Support the tail with the revolving centre. Skim the surface of the blank with a gouge.

- Using the template as a guide, mark all the main points on the revolving bobbin blank in pencil. *(Fig.15.2).*

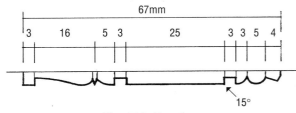

Fig. 15.2. Template.

Fig. 15.1. Fairing bobbin.

- Turn the tail, wire grooves, collars and shaping as described earlier.

- When the body shaping and wire grooves are finished the spiral groove may be cut.

- Take a junior hacksaw, remove the blade then replace it with the teeth facing backwards. This prevents it from cutting aggressively allowing more control.

- Place the saw on the wire groove (tailstock end) at a 15 degree angle. To do this hold the saw at 90 degrees to the bobbin with the saw blade resting in the groove. Next move the hand holding the hacksaw towards the tailstock so that the blade is set at the correct angle. It may be helpful to mark that angle upon the card template and use it as a guide in the future. *(Fig. 15.3).*

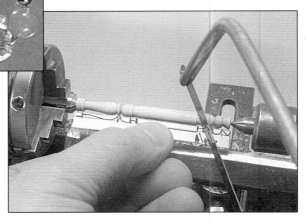

Fig. 15.3. Setting the saw to 15 degrees.

- Move the saw backwards and forwards lightly at that angle. Using the left hand, slowly rotate the chuck anti-clockwise which is the normal rotation of the chuck. Keep the saw moving backwards and forwards at that angle and it will be noticed that this combination of the slow rotation of the work and the angled cut of the saw produces a regular spiral cut. Stop when the saw blade reaches the headstock wire groove. *(Fig. 15.4).*

Fig. 15.4. Cutting the spiral.

● The groove can be widened out using a file if desired. It is more convenient to use a pendant drill (or Dremel tool) fitted with a flat fissure burr. This burr is exactly the same tool as used by a Dentist. *(Fig. 15.7)*. The spiral saw cut groove will act as a guide.

Fig. 15.5. Starting the spiral cut.

● Switch the pendant drill on and hold the rotating burr above the start of the saw cut matching the angle. Slowly lower the rotating burr bringing it into contact with the guiding angled saw cut. Rotate the chuck by hand as before, maintaining the angle of the burr following the saw cut pathway. A regular deepish groove will be cut from one wire groove to the next. *(Fig. 15.5 &15.6)*.

Practice may be needed to maintain a regular cut and to keep the rotating burr in the guide groove. Sometimes the burr will try to jump out of the groove, practice on less valuable pieces of work will provide the experience to prevent this from happening.

● When satisfied with the shape of the bobbin and the spiral groove, *(Fig. 15.8)*. lightly glass-paper (don't knock off the sharp edges) and then polish.

● In preparation for decoration take a 1mm ($^1/_{24}$ inch) drill and drill into the tail for the spangle, then drill at the base of the tail end wire groove and the top of the head wire groove.

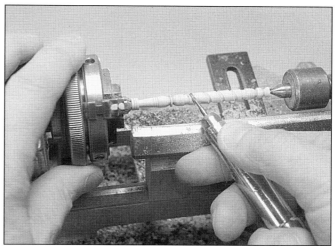

Fig. 15.6. Finishing the cut with the burr.

● Set the bobbin aside ready for the tinsel and wire decoration which is described in a later chapter.

Fig. 15.8. The completed cut and burr.   *Fig. 15.7. The flat fissure burr.*

16 – Brass Pin Inlay.
(Made In Rosewood).

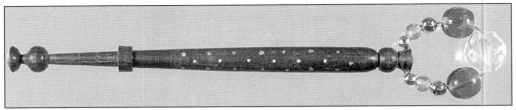

Fig. 16.1. Brass pin bobbin.

Brass pin inlay may be seen as decoration on many early pieces of treen so it is not unusual to see this form of decoration upon lace bobbins. Used as an overall pattern it is not rare but when used to spell out names or dates it is less common. One major problem that occurs in this form of decoration is corrosion of the pins, which in turn may split the bobbin, but that of course takes many years. I think that some early bobbin makers did understand the problem of metal corrosion for there are some fine examples of bobbins with patterns of inlaid thorns. The thorns were used like wooden pins producing patterns which have remained intact even after 150 years of use.

For this modern pin inlay bobbin I have chosen to use Rosewood. Those tiny golden pin pricks of reflected light can look like sparking stars against the rich black night sky. *(Fig. 16.1).*

● Having turned the head and neck, which are now held in collets in the headstock, turn the tail and the body to the simple shape shown on the template. *(Fig.16.2).*

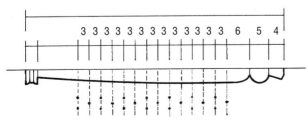

Fig. 16.2. Template.

● On the template points 0 — 12 are shown. Each point is 3mm ($^1/_8$ inch) apart. Line 0 being set 15mm ($^5/_8$ inch) from the bobbin collar closest to the chuck.

● With the lathe running carefully and accurately transfer the marks 0 — 12 to the body of the bobbin. *(Fig. 16.3).*

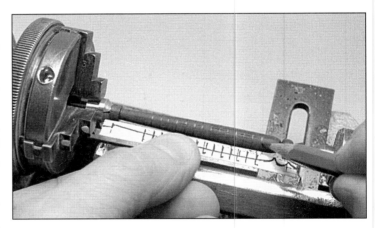

Fig. 16.3. Transferring the marks to the bobbin.

When marking on dark woods it may be easier to use a white pencil crayon. Sharpen it to a good point so that the line is seen clearly.

● Switch off the lathe and bring one chuck jaw to 12 o'clock and use it as an index.

Fig. 16.4. Drawing the "top" line.

Fig. 16.5. Drilling the holes.

- Mark a line across the top of the bobbin between 0 and 12. *(Fig. 16.4).*

- Move the chuck jaw to the 3 o'clock position. Mark a second line along the top of the bobbin from 0 to 12.

- Move the chuck jaw to the 6 o'clock position marking a third line along the top of the bobbin from 0 to 12.

- Next move the chuck jaw to 9 o'clock and again mark a line from 0 to 12.

- Finally mark four more lines but this time set the index chuck jaw between positions 12 and 3, 3 and 6, 6 and 9, 9 and 12. This will divide the bobbin into eight vertical segments.

- Into the pendant drill fit a fine drill. The size of the drill should match the diameter of the brass pins being used. (About 0.75mm or $^1/_{32}$ inch.)

- Arrange the bobbin in the lathe so that one of the lengthwise lines is at the top.

- Switch the pendant drill on and drill vertically at positions 0,2,4,6,8,10 and 12 to about half the thickness of the bobbin. *(Fig. 16.5).*

- Take a brass pin, a tube of Supaglue (crazy glue) and a pair of fine wire cutters. Nail clippers will work just as well.

- Apply a small amount of glue to the tip of the pin and push it into the first hole (position 0). *(Fig. 16.6).*

- Clip off close to the bobbin leaving about 1mm ($^1/_{24}$ inch) showing. *(Fig. 16.7).*

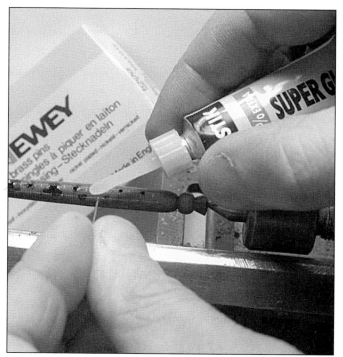

Fig. 16.6. Gluing the pins.

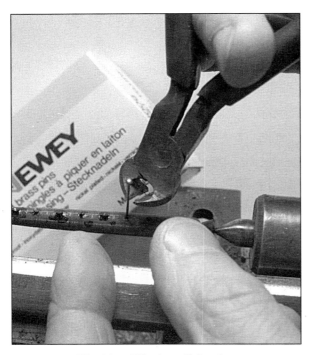

Fig. 16.7. Clipping off the pins.

● Move to each of the other holes, gluing the pin, pushing it into the hole and clipping off. Do not use the last part of the pin with the head attached, discard that.

● Having glued, fitted and clipped the pins to the first line move to the second but this time drill the positions 1,3,5,7,9, and 11 to the same depth.

● Glue pins in each hole and clip off.

● At the next line drill the even numbered holes, glue in pins and clip off. The following line drill odd numbered holes, glue pins and clip. Next line drill and fit even numbers, next line odd numbers and so on until the bobbin looks like a startled Hedgehog.

● Leave the bobbin for an hour to fully dry.

The reason for drilling and filling each line before moving to the next is simple. If all the holes were drilled first, as the pins were glued and fitted many of the open holes around the bobbin would become clogged with glue, so work in an orderly fashion, one line at a time and all should proceed satisfactorily.

● When completely satisfied that all the glue has dried take a medium fine file and begin to file the pins level with the wood surface. File slowly and carefully so that the pins are not pushed out of their drilled holes. *(Fig. 16.8).*

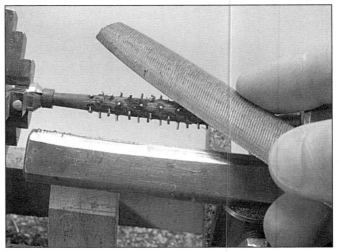

Fig.16.8. The pins are filed smooth.

● If the pins are dislodged re-drill the hole, glue a fresh pin in place and clip off.

● When the pins are all filed flush use fine glass-paper to clean the whole of the bobbin bringing a sparkle to the pin dots.

● Finally make sure that the surface is clean of all file marks then polish to a high shine. *(Fig. 16.9).*

Fig. 16.9. Sparkling like stars in a night sky.

17 – Wired Loose Ring.
(Made From Sandalwood.)

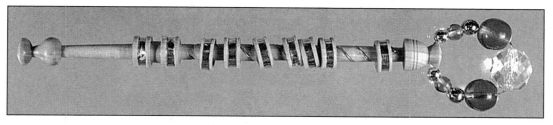

Fig. 17.1. Loose ring bobbin.

The most splendid loose ringed lace bobbin I have ever seen was made over 150 years ago by Joseph Haskins of Bedford. It was worked in bone upon a treadle lathe and had seven loose rings each one laid over with gold leaf. The loose rings ran upon a centre spindle which had been decorated with a spiral of wire and tinsel looking like a miniature barbers pole.

Although not the most practical of lace bobbins it is a fine piece to make. Here I will show how it is made from a piece of West Australian Sandalwood. The rings will be bound with gold coloured, paper backed, tinsel — of course you may use gold leaf if you wish. The centre spindle is wrapped with two twists of brass wire. Joseph Haskins underlaid his wire with tinsel. You will understand having used only wire why only those with considerable experience in decorating with tinsel would wish to try.

> *Prepare the blank as for a basic bobbin, turning head and neck. Make sure the blank is a generous 9mm ($^3/8$ inch) diameter. Hold the head and neck in the collets in the chuck supporting the tail end with the revolving centre. Skim the blank so that it runs true and clean. Use a pencil to transfer the main points from the template to the rotating blank. Eight loose rings are marked. (Fig.17.2).*

● Two special tools are needed for this particular bobbin. One is a square end tool 2mm ($^1/12$ inch) wide. This can be ground out from a cheap wood chisel.

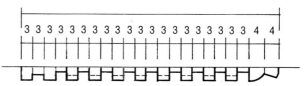

Fig.17.2. Template.

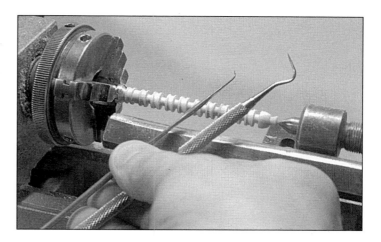

Fig. 17.3. Crochet hook and dental pick.

● The second tool, to be used to undercut the rings, is made from a 0.6 metal crochet hook. Cut or break off the hook then carefully bend about 3mm ($^1/8$ inch) of the end to a 45 degree angle. The outer edges can be ground and the inner edges sharpened using an oil stone to the profile shown in the diagram. This will allow it to cut left and right. It may be sensible to practice with this tool first to ensure that it works well and that you can use it proficiently. Adjustments may be made to the cutting edges to improve its performance having studied the cut it has produced. *(Figs. 17.3, 17.4 & 17.5).*

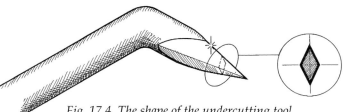

Fig. 17.4. The shape of the undercutting tool.

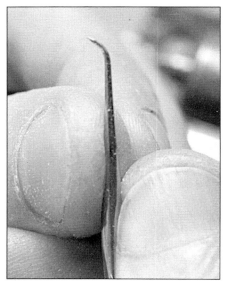

Fig. 17.5. The bent end of the crochet hook.

- Using the square end tool shape the tail.

- Next work on the two mock rings at the chuck end.

- A 9mm ($^3/_8$ inch) area is left for these two mock rings and is marked out in three 3mm ($^1/_8$ inch) sections. The middle section is turned out down to 4mm ($^1/_6$ inch) diameter.

- In the centre of each of the remaining areas use the 2mm ($^1/_{12}$ inch) Y. square end tool and cut a groove 1mm ($^1/_{24}$ inch) deep. As can be seen this leaves a small raised area each side of the groove.

- Take the skew chisel and clean off the end of the tail and shape the curved end down to the tail.

- Using the corner of the square end tool cut two incised lines into the curved end of the tail for decoration.

- Now we move on to cut the rings free.

- Use the fine square end tool to turn away the waste wood between the rings. Move the tool slightly from side to side to prevent it from gripping, cutting down to an even bottomed 4mm ($^1/_6$ inch) diameter and 3mm ($^1/_8$ inch) wide groove.

- Use the narrow 2mm ($^1/_{12}$ inch) square end tool to cut a shallow, 1mm ($^1/_{24}$ inch) deep, groove in the middle of each "ring". This area will be decorated with gold coloured tinsel. (Fig. 17.6).

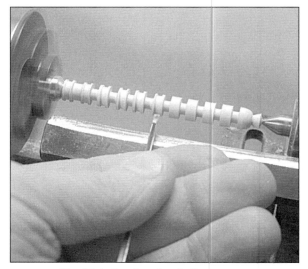

Fig. 17.6. Cutting the shallow groove.

- Now polish all the rings before they are cut free, for once they are loose they will be very difficult to polish.

- Working from the tailstock end take the crochet hook/undercutting tool and make the first cut from the right moving the tool into the "ring" so that it follows a "natural" pathway. This will become apparent when using the tool for there will be an area where it cuts more easily and freely. Widen out that area with a second lower cut. (Fig. 17.7).

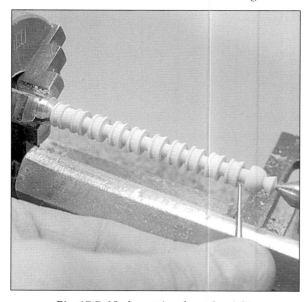

Fig. 17.7. Undercutting from the right.

- Do not force these cuts for pressure can shatter the ring.

- When the undercut from the right is sufficiently wide and deep move the tool to the left of the ring and begin the undercut from that side. Again find the "natural" and easy cut for the tool, widen the cut preventing it from grabbing.

- The two cuts from either side should meet below the ring allowing it to run free. If it can be moved towards the right do so. If not use the undercutting tool to work away at the waste wood beneath until it can be moved. Clean up the cut area on the spindle using a square end tool.

- The first ring, now free, is moved to the right and held against the tail end using a piece of masking tape. This will prevent it working its way towards the second ring and interfering with the work. (Fig. 17.8).

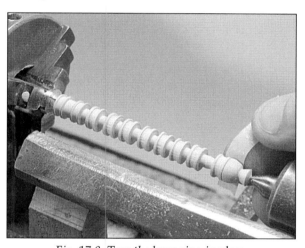

Fig. 17.8. Tape the loose ring in place.

Some points to consider when cutting the rings. Try to ensure that the undercutting tool runs parallel to the centre spindle — do not allow it to cut down into that spindle for it will reduce its diameter and weaken it.

The undercutting tool's length obviously has to be more than half the ring's width, so make sure when bending that a full 3mm ($^1/_8$ inch) is bent.

- Continue working all the rings in this manner. Rings 3, 4 and 5 will be the most difficult for they are in the middle and the thin centre spindle may begin to flex. Just cut more steadily and all will be well. (Fig. 17.9).

Fig. 17.9. Undercutting from the left.

- When all the rings have been cut move them all to the right and hold in place with masking tape. Clean down the centre spindle to an even 3mm ($^1/_8$ inch) diameter. Polish the whole of that end of the spindle.

- Move the rings to the left and hold them in place so that the remaining part of the centre spindle may be turned to diameter and polished. Leave the rings held at the headstock end for the time being.

- All that remains is to cut the two twist wire grooves.

- Bring one chosen chuck jaw to 12 o'clock. Take a junior hacksaw with the blade set backwards and place it on the centre spindle, at the tailstock end, held at 45 degrees. Turn the chuck anti-clockwise by hand whilst moving the saw backwards and forwards at that angle. This will cut a spiral groove. Halt when close to the loose rings.

Fig. 17.10. Sawing the wire groove.

- Remove the saw and move the chosen index jaw to 6 o'clock. Place the saw back on the spindle (at the tailstock end) again at 45 degrees, repeating the spiral cut. This will create a second parallel spiral groove. (Fig. 17.10).

- Move the loose rings to the tailstock end and tape them in place. If the rings cover the start of the groove move a few rings back to the headstock end and tape them in place. When the spiral cuts reach them move them back towards the tail end.

- To continue cutting the spiral grooves bring the end of one cut to top dead centre placing the saw in the cut and at 45 degrees to the work. Again turn the chuck using the left hand whilst moving the saw backwards and forwards until the mock rings at the headstock end are reached. Do not cut into those rings.

- Repeat the process to cut the second groove but the starting point will be set 180 degrees away from the first.

- The centre spindle and the rest of the bobbin may now be fully polished.

- If a 1mm ($^1/_{24}$ inch) hole is drilled vertically through the start and finish of either groove it should break through into the other.

- Remove the finished bobbin from the lathe to begin the decoration. Hold the bobbin with the head towards the right.

- To wire the first groove move all the rings to the extreme right.

- Take a 150mm (3 inch) length of 26 gauge soft temper bright drawn brass wire.

- Bend a 3mm ($^1/_8$ inch) right angled hook in one end. Hold the other end temporarily in a vice.

- Place the bent end into the drilled wire hole at the left hand end.

- Hold the bobbin at 45 degrees so that the wire follows the groove. Turn the bobbin in the hands so that the wire drops into the groove. When the wire reaches the loose rings maintain the tension but release the end from the vice. (Fig. 17.11).

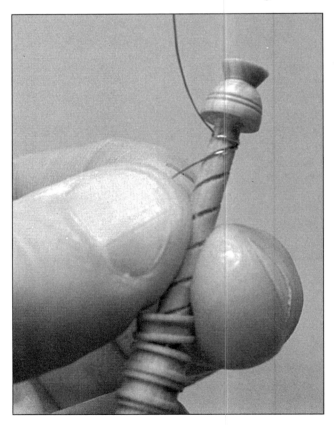

Fig. 17.11. The wire decoration is begun.

- Carefully thread the released end under the loose rings sliding them along yet maintaining tension on the wire. (Fig. 17.12).

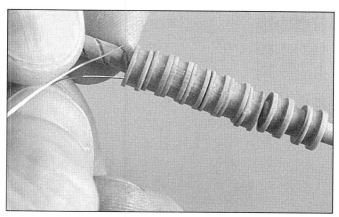

Fig. 17.12. Threading the wire under the rings.

- When all the loose rings are at the left-hand end replace the wire end in the vice and continue winding it into the groove.

- When the end of the first groove is reached release the wire from the vice but maintain the tension. Thread the end through the drilled hole and pull it tight. *(Fig. 17.13).*

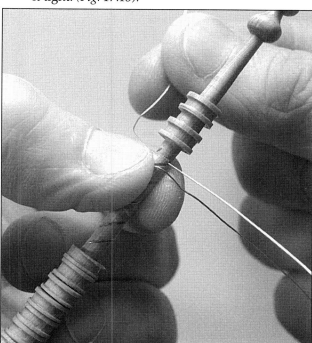

Fig. 17.13. The wire is threaded through the end hole.

- Replace the wire end in the vice and run the wire into the second groove but now moving in the opposite direction.

- When the rings are reached remove the wire from the vice, maintaining tension, then thread the wire under the rings. *(Fig. 17.14).*

- Move the rings along the now wire decorated spindle replace the end of the wire in the vice and continue winding it into the spiral groove.

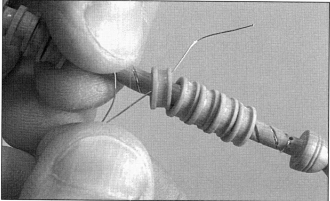

Fig. 17.14. Threading the wire back under the rings.

- When the end of that groove is reached remove the wire, for the last time, from the vice and clip the bent end off.

- Thread the now clean end of the wire into the drilled hole (partially filled with the first end of the wire) pull tightly through then clip off close. *(Fig. 17.15).*

Now that you understand the difficulty of wiring this style you will also understand the greater difficulty which would be encountered if the underlying spiral groove were decorated with tinsel.

- Drill the tail ready for spangling.

For details of applying the gold coloured tinsel to the loose rings refer to the chapter on decorating bobbins.

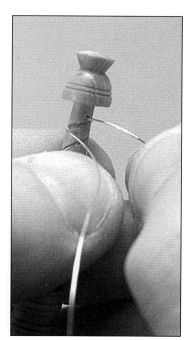

Fig. 17.15. Finishing off.

18 – Double Fairing.
(Made In Mahonia.)

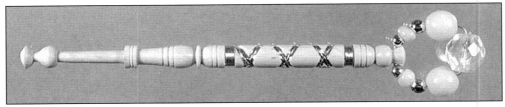

Fig. 18.1. Double fairing.

The double fairing is a most interesting form of decoration using a right handed and a left handed spiral groove each filled with coloured tinsel and crossing one another regularly, creating a plaid form of pattern. The most important feature in creating a successful double fairing is to maintain regular angles left and right ensuring that the intersections fall equally.

● With the blank held in the chuck, head held in the collets and tail supported with a revolving centre mark the main points from the template. *(Fig.18.2).*

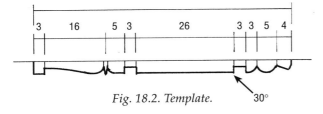

Fig. 18.2. Template.   30°

● Turn the basic body shape and the two wire grooves.

● Use one chuck jaw as an index and bring it to 12 o'clock. Mark a pencil line along the length of the bobbin from one wire groove to the next.

● Turn the chuck so that the index is now at 6 o'clock and mark another pencil line from one wire groove to the next on the top of the bobbin. Remember if the wood is dark use a white pencil crayon.

● Take a junior hacksaw with the blade set backwards in the frame. Place the blade where the pencil line touches the right hand wire groove. Move the hacksaw so that it is set at 30 degrees to the bobbin. *(Fig. 18.3).*

● Begin moving the saw backwards and forwards at that angle and at the same time, using the left hand, turning the chuck anti-clockwise. Stop when the wire groove is reached. The first right hand spiral has been cut.

Fig. 18.3. Setting the saw to 30 degrees.

● To set the angle for the return left hand spiral place the saw blade where the saw cut crosses the pencil line closest to the left hand wire groove. *(Fig. 18.4).*

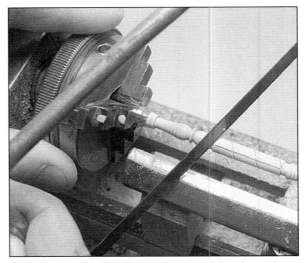

Fig. 18.4. Setting the saw for the left hand spiral.

- The chuck will be turned, using the left hand, rotating anti-clockwise as before. Test by rolling the blade on the surface, (not cutting) from that first intersection, to the next intersection of the spiral cut and the pencil line halfway around the bobbin. Adjust the angle of the blade until it moves smoothly from one intersection to the next. Maintaining that angle work from the position where the right hand saw cut meets the left hand wire groove and begin to cut the left hand spiral hitting each intersection until the right hand wire groove is reached.

- This left hand spiral will be a little difficult for right handed workers but practice will improve the skill.

- The left and right hand spiral guide cuts have been made. *(Fig. 18.5)*. Now to widen them to accept the coloured tinsel.

Fig. 18.5. The left hand spiral is cut.

- Into the pendant drill (of course you may use fine files to widen the groove) fit a flat fissure burr.

- Starting at the headstock end align the burr to the start of the left hand spiral guide groove.

- Hold the burr above the cut line at exactly the same angle. Switch on, bring the rotating burr down to cut into the cut line, slowly rotate the lathe by hand and follow the guide cut. A left hand spiral groove will now have been cut, stop at the right hand wire groove. *(Fig. 18.6)*.

Fig. 18.6. Using the burr to widen the left hand spiral.

- Now readjust the burr so that it is aligned with the start of the right hand spiral guide groove at the right hand wire groove. Bring the rotating burr down to cut following the guide line whilst rotating the chuck. Take particular care at intersections, work carefully until the left hand wire groove is reached then halt. *(Fig. 18.7)*.

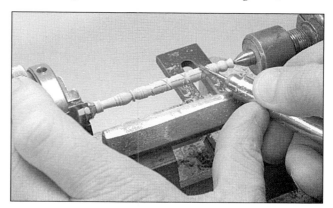

Fig. 18.7. Widening the right hand spiral.

- Clean up the grooves using a round needle file, glasspaper the whole bobbin lightly then polish.

- Finally drill the tail for a spangle remembering how the decoration will lie in relation to the spangle.

- So that the bobbin can be decorated with wire and tinsel drill a fine hole at the base and top of the right hand wire groove, and the base and top of the left hand wire groove.

- Refer to the section on decorating bobbins for a full explanation of how the bobbin is wired and tinselled.

19 – Beaded.
(Made In Olivewood.)

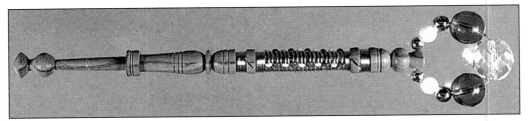

Fig. 19.1. Beaded bobbin.

These fine bead decorated bobbins were a favourite of many bobbinmakers for many patterns could be created by altering the colour and position of the beads. Here I will show a simple method of bead decoration using three channels in which the beads are "dropped" off. Even so by altering the colours of the beads many variations on this simple theme may be achieved.

● Upon the blank held in the lathe mark the major points from the template. *(Fig.19.2).*

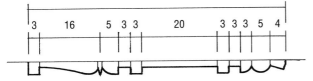

Fig. 19.2. Template.

● Turn the basic bobbin shape but this time between the two wire grooves turn a wide groove. This wide groove should be about 1.5mm ($^1/_{16}$ inch) deep.

● Use the chuck jaws (3 in number) as index positions. Bring the first jaw to 12 o'clock.

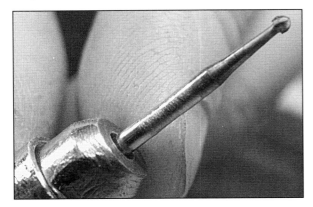

Fig. 19.3. A round end burr.

● Fit a 1.5mm ($^1/_{16}$ inch) diameter round end burr into the pendant drill. Make sure it is set well out so about 30mm (1 $^1/_4$ inch) of the burrs shaft is showing. *(Fig. 19.3).*

● Set the tool rest so that the burr, when resting upon it, is exactly at centre height. *(Fig. 19.4).*

● With the burr rotating, and set at the left hand end of the wide groove, push it into the bobbin and draw it steadily along the tool rest cutting a straight groove. When the burr reaches the right hand end of the groove switch off.

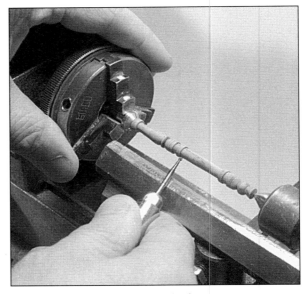

Fig. 19.4. Running the first groove.

● Move the second jaw to 12 o'clock and repeat the cut using the burr.

● When that groove has been worked move the third jaw to 12 o'clock and cut a third Channel down the length of the central wire groove. *(Fig. 19.5).*

Fig. 19.5. All the grooves cut.

● Bring one cut groove to 12 o'clock and make a saw cut at about 45 degrees from the left hand wire groove across the wood separating it and the central wide groove. Move to the right hand wire groove and make a similar cut linking it to the central wide groove. *(Fig. 19.6).*

Fig. 19.6.
45° saw cut links the wire groove to the decoration area.

● Lightly glass-paper then polish.

● Using a fine drill, drill the headstock end of the left hand wire groove and the tailstock end of the right hand wire groove. When drilling the tail for a spangle hole consider how the decorated bobbin will lie upon the lace pillow.

● The section on decorating bobbins will have a description of bead decorating a bobbin shank.

Fig. 19.7.
Mother & Babe with bead decoration.

Fig. 19.8. An antique bobbin showing beads run in a spiral groove.

Fig. 19.9 "A Bedfordshire lacemaker."

20 – Cow And Calf.
(Made In Tulipwood And Kingwood.)

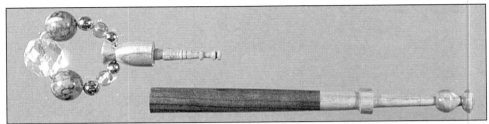

Fig. 20.1. Cow and calf apart.

Tricks and hidden pieces have always been popular amongst bobbinmakers. Unfortunately age and wear has caused many of the early bobbins with cunningly concealed parts either to have jammed firmly in place or to have loosened and fallen apart. The cow and calf is a traditional form of bobbin which outwardly looks quite plain but has a hidden secret. Pulled apart there is a tiny bobbin, the calf, attached to the bobbin tail end.

Here I will describe how to make a simple but effective cow and calf which should, if made carefully, neither jam nor fall apart through wear. An internal groove is cut into the main part of the bobbin and a corresponding bulb is turned on the base of the calf. The bulb is an interference fit in the hollow, clicking into place in the internal groove, to be firmly held.

- One simple special tool is needed and that may be ground from a cheap 6mm ($^1/_4$ inch) wood chisel. A small hockey stick end is required. For precise size and shape refer to the sketch. *(Fig.20.2).*

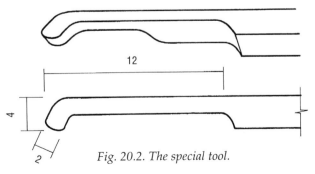

12

4

2

Fig. 20.2. The special tool.

- The bobbin is made from three separate pieces. The first, for the head and neck, is 45mm ($1^3/_4$ inch) long. The second, the middle, is 40mm

(1 $^5/_8$ inch) long. The third, the calf, is 30mm (1 $^1/_4$ inch) long. All are cut from prepared pieces of 6mm ($^1/_4$ inch) dowel. Pieces one and three have been cut from Tulipwood. The middle piece has been cut from Kingwood. *(Fig. 20.4.).*

- Take the Kingwood piece and hold it in the chuck with a little showing. Square off the end.

- Fit a drill chuck holding a 3mm ($^1/_8$ inch) drill to the tailstock and drill into the Kingwood to a depth of about 20mm ($^{13}/_{16}$ inch). *(Fig. 20.3).*

Fig. 20.3. Drilling out the centre.

- Switch off the lathe and remove the Kingwood piece, turn it around and replace it in the chuck so that the undrilled end faces front. Square off and drill through until the first hole is reached. Remove the piece from the chuck and set aside.

- Take the first piece (Tulipwood) and hold it in the chuck with about 9mm ($^3/_8$ inch) showing.

- Square off the end and turn a 3mm ($^1/_8$ inch) spigot 6mm ($^1/_4$ inch) long.

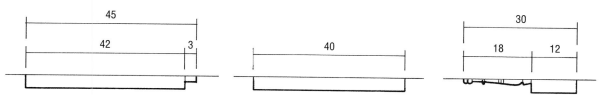

Fig. 20.4. Templates for the three parts.

- Remove from the chuck and replace with the third piece, also Tulipwood, leaving about 20mm ($^{13}/_{16}$ inch) showing.

- Bring up the tailstock holding a revolving centre to support the end. From the tailstock end measure 12mm ($^{1}/_{2}$ inch) followed by 3mm ($^{1}/_{8}$ inch) and a further 3mm ($^{1}/_{8}$ inch). At each of these positions mark a pencil line.

- Turn the 12mm ($^{1}/_{2}$ inch) length just under 3mm ($^{1}/_{8}$ inch) diameter.

- Leave the next 3mm ($^{1}/_{8}$ inch) section larger than the 3mm ($^{1}/_{8}$ inch) diameter. Call this part the bulb. *(Fig. 20.5).*

- Turn the final 3mm ($^{1}/_{8}$ inch) section just below 3mm ($^{1}/_{8}$ inch) diameter.

Fig. 20.5. Measuring the bulb.

- Now return to the bulb. Do not reduce its diameter yet but turn from the tailstock and sweep up into that bulb leaving a ramp with only a narrow section full diameter. *(Fig. 20.7).*

- Using a skew chisel round off the back of that bulb close to the chuck. *(Fig.20.6.).* Rub a little candle wax on the bulb.

- Take the middle section (Kingwood) which has been drilled out. Withdraw the tailstock, push the drilled out middle section onto the part- turned "calf". Test the bulb carefully in the drilled hole.

Fig. 20.6. Turning the calf.

- The aim is to make it an interference fit, but not so tight that it will split the middle, and not so loose that it will fall out. The bulb may be reduced in diameter with careful use of glass-paper.

- When satisfied with the fit bring the revolving centre back to support the end of the calf. Do not turn the bulb again.

- Using a fine skew chisel or a fine square end tool shape the tail of the calf close to the chuck below the bulb.

- Turn the head and neck of the calf using a small skew chisel.

- A small square end tool may be used to turn the collar and part of the body. Mark a few incised lines on the body then lightly glass-paper and polish.

- Complete with a rub of wax on the bulb.

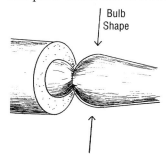

Bulb Shape

Fig. 20.7.
The bulb shape.

Fitting The Calf Into The Main Body.

- Take the drilled out Kingwood piece and hold it in the chuck with a little overhanging. Bring the tool rest across the face of the work.

- Set the specially shaped hockey stick tool so that the "hockey" end lines up with the bulb. *(Fig. 20.8)*. Make a mark on the tool (use typist correction fluid) which corresponds with the shoulder of the calf.

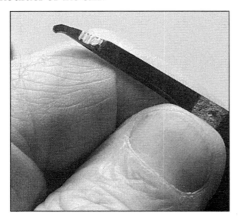

Fig. 20.8. The hockey stick tool.

- Switch the lathe on, take the special tool placing it on the tool rest then push it into the revolving hole. Make sure that it does not cut into the work until the depth mark is reached. *(Fig. 20.9)*.

Fig. 20.9. Undercutting the internal groove.

- Move the cutting end of the special tool against the revolving interior cutting an internal groove. When satisfied that the internal groove is sufficiently deep and well shaped remove the tool from the work. Switch the lathe off, withdraw the tool rest and test the calf in the hollow for fit. There should be a satisfying click as the bulb drops and locks into the internal groove. *(Fig.20.10)*.

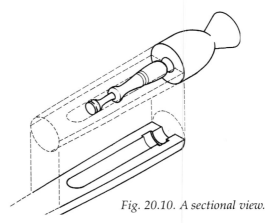

Fig. 20.10. A sectional view.

- If the fit is slack one more chance is allowed. Remove the piece from the chuck, turn it around replace it in the chuck and turn another groove — precisely this time.

- When the calf fits well leave it in place. Take the first piece and glue the small spigot then push that glued end into the centre Kingwood piece. (Do not use very runny glue which might run towards the calf.)

- Hold the parts in the lathe using the tailstock to add pressure whilst the glue sets.

- Once the glue has dried turn the head and neck as you would for any other wooden bobbin. Then hold the head and neck in the brass collets in the chuck so that the body may be turned. *(Fig.20.11)*.

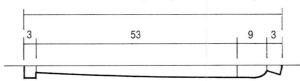

Fig. 20.11. Template.

- I prefer to turn the bobbin plainly leaving the interest in the secret "calf". If more ornamented turning is decided upon remember the internal hollow and the position where the calf enters avoiding turning too deeply which would weaken the bobbin. *(Fig. 20.12)*.

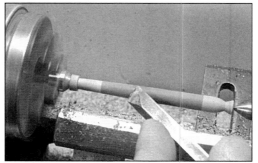

Fig. 20.12. Turning the body.

21 – Pewter Inlaid Bobbins.
(Made In Rosewood.)

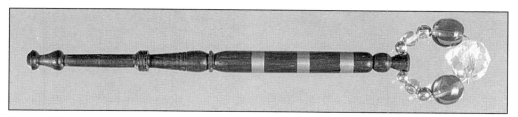

Fig. 21.1. Pewter tiger.

*I*t must be understood that there are dangers involved with the process of pewter inlay. Molten metal can cause serious burns and can also cause fires. The fumes given off by the molten pewter will contain lead so the area will need to be well ventilated. The mould used must be kept dry and care must be taken when using resinous woods.

Butterflies, Tigers and Leopards are the very descriptive names of pewter inlaid bobbins. The Leopard has spots, the Tiger has stripes and the Butterfly has wings. The decoration is cut into the bobbin body and then the molten pewter is poured in.

When I began searching for information to discover how the early bobbinmakers cast their pewter into bobbins I could find only one reference. That described the mould as being made from stone. I took this to mean fired clay or pottery.

Although I made a mould from clay I found that the best and most long lasting material was car body filler. My original mould still works well and has the date 1977 scratched into its side.

● To make a mould you will need the following: — some Plasticine, pieces of card, a 6mm ($^1/_4$ inch) diameter dowel, car body filler and a little talcum powder.

● It can be seen in the illustration *(Fig.21.2)* that Plasticine or clay has been moulded to shape, two index lugs have been moulded, a dowel has been laid in place and four pieces of card fixed around the edge.

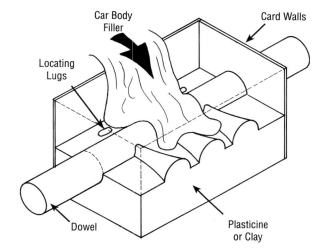

Fig. 21.2. Making the mould.

● The dowel and the surface of the mould is dusted with talcum powder. This will prevent the car body filler permanently sticking to those parts.

● Pour the car body filler into the mould tapping the edges to shake air bubbles to the surface.

● Remember that when car body filler is curing heat is produced, this may melt some types of Plasticine.

● When the filler has set take the mould apart, clean off the Plasticine, remove the dowel and then tidy up the surface filling in small air holes with a fresh mix of filler.

● To make the second half of the mould fit the dowel in place, build up the pouring channels with Plasticine or clay, fix card sides around the mould then dust the inside with talcum powder. Pour in the car body filler and leave it to dry.

● When the filler has set separate the two halves, clean up the pouring channel in the new half and fill in any small air holes with fresh filler.

● Allow the finished mould to cure thoroughly before it is used. *(Fig. 21.3).*

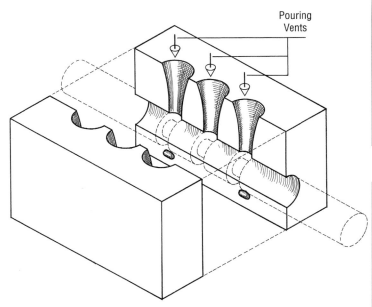

Fig. 21.3. The mould.

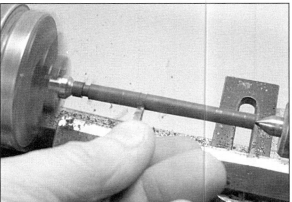

Fig. 21.4. Turning the tiger grooves.

Fig. 21.5. Cutting the "key" in the groove.

The three styles of pewter inlay, Butterfly, Tiger and Leopard each require different grooves or recesses cut into the bobbin body to accept the molten metal. All three need the grooves to line up with the pouring channels in the mould.

For each of the bobbins the head and neck of the blank is first turned then the grooves or recesses are cut into the dowel body. The dowel needs to be a precise 6mm ($^1/_4$ inch) diameter.

I will deal with the preparation of each in turn then discuss the casting as a single process.

Tiger. *(Fig. 21.1)*

Using a square end tool turn three 1.5mm ($^1/_{16}$ inch) deep, flat bottomed grooves in the position marked from the template. *(Fig. 21.4)*. To prevent the cast rings from rotating loosely around the grooves a simple "key" is cut into the groove base. Use a junior hacksaw to make two light cuts angled towards one another in the groove. This should be sufficient to lock the solidified pewter ring in place. *(Fig.21.5).*

Butterfly. *(Fig. 21.12)*

Turn three grooves as for the tiger but use a flat fissure burr to cut two wings on either side of the centre channel. These wings slope down and away to form an arrow shape. Another set of "wings" are cut on the opposite side. *(Fig.21.6 & Fig.21.7).*

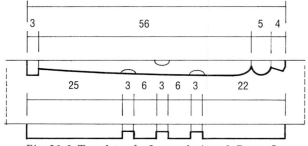

Fig. 21.6. Templates for Leopard, tiger & Butterfly.

Fig. 21.7. Cutting the Butterfly "wings".

Leopard. *(Fig. 21.10)*

At each of the three marked position on the dowel body drill a 2mm ($^1/_{12}$ inch) hole. The middle hole is drilled so that it sits at 90 degrees to the outer two. Countersink both sides of all the holes. This will form a more interesting, larger outer dot and have two effects — first it will not weaken the bobbin with a large hole drilled through yet will give that appearance and second the countersink either side will act as a key to hold the cast metal in place. *(Fig.21.8).*

Fig. 21.8. Countersinking the Leopard spots.

Casting the pewter.

Now a secret — I do not use pewter. I use common Plumbers solder. In fact having had the pewter from bobbins which were made in the 1850s analysed I discovered that the better, high quality pewter (that with a high tin content) developed tin plague, it corroded badly and the bobbins which were inlaid with it became unusable. Bobbins made with poor quality pewter (having a high lead content which would be very much like solder) have survived intact.

- Quickly and lightly play the gas flame over the inside of the mould to warm it and also to burn off any moisture.

- Place the blank in the mould aligning the turned grooves with the pouring vents. Make sure that when viewed from above the grooves may be seen at the base of the pouring vents.

Fig. 21.9. The mould.

- Hold the mould in a vice. Have a sand tray on the floor beneath the mould to catch any spilt molten solder.

- In a well ventilated room, wearing eye protection, heat proof gloves and a substantial apron melt the solder in a metal dish using the gas torch. *(Fig. 21.11).*

- Carefully pour the molten solder into the mould until it

Fig. 21.10. Pewter Leopard.

Fig. 21.11. Heating the pewter over a gas torch.

Fig. 21.12. Pewter Butterfly.

rises to the top of the pouring vents then stop. (Fig. 21.13).

Fig. 21.13. Pouring the molten metal.

● Leave the blank in the mould until the molten solder has set. When cool remove the mould from the vice. Open the mould to reveal the cast bobbin.

● Hold the pouring vent cast block in the vice then carefully, using a hacksaw, saw it from the blank. Rub candle wax on the hacksaw teeth to prevent them from gripping. (Fig. 21.14).

Fig. 21.14. Cutting off the excess "pewter".

● If there are any minor flaws in the casting use a soldering iron to infill.

● Return the blank to the lathe holding the head and neck in collets in the chuck. Support the tail using the revolving centre.

● Carefully file the excess "pewter" away. Next glass-paper the surface. (Fig. 21.15).

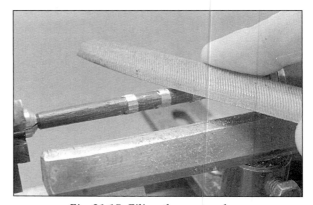

Fig. 21.15. Filing the pewter clean.

● Turn the bobbin as normal but do not turn the pewter for it can easily be torn out. Finish the area around the pewter using wire wool rubbing along the bobbin body. When the pewter has a high lustre and the bobbin is well finished, polish. (Fig. 21.16).

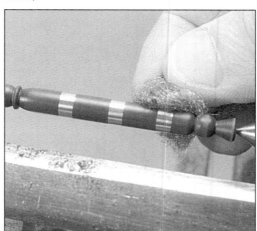

Fig. 21.16. Finishing with wire wool.

22 – Inlaid Bobbins.
(Made Using A Variety Of Materials.)

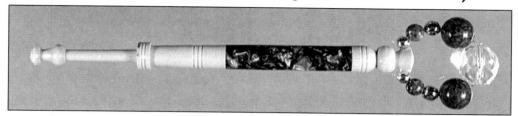

Fig. 22.1. Crushed velvet inlay.

Some woods or other materials, although most attractive, do not lend themselves to bobbin making. These materials are either too brittle, too open grained, too soft or completely unsuitable because of their construction for example Tunbridge mosaic.

The following method overcomes the problem for a good, close grained, wood will be used for the top and tail, the more attractive piece displayed between. It really is a most exciting method of producing bobbins for any conceivable centre may be used.

For convenience this section is split into two parts.
1. Solid centres such as burrwood and plastics.
2. Constructed centres e.g.. Tunbridge mosaic.

1. Solid Centres.

Here for the solid centres I have used are Turu (or palmwood), Blue Gum Burr, Beefwood, Dymondwood (a coloured laminated wood), Mahonia and a plastic material called Crushed Velvet *(Fig. 22.1)* from which pen bodies are turned. At the end of this section I will discuss the various turning properties of these materials.

Preparation.

- Cut two pieces of close grained wood, one 56mm (2 ^{1}/$_4$ inch) long by 9mm (^{3}/$_8$ inch) square for the top. The second piece is 24mm (1 inch) long by 9mm (^{3}/$_8$ inch) square for the tail.

- Turn both pieces round as close to 6mm (^{1}/$_4$ inch) diameter as possible.

- Holding each piece at a time in the chuck turn a 6mm (^{1}/$_4$ inch) long by 3mm (^{1}/$_8$ inch) diameter

spigot on one end making sure that the shoulders are turned square. Then set these pieces to one side. *(Fig. 22.2).*

Fig. 22.2. Turning the spigot.

- Take a 45mm (2 ^{3}/$_4$ inch) length by 9mm (^{3}/$_8$ inch) square piece of the chosen centre. Turn it fully round as close to 6mm (^{1}/$_4$ inch) diameter. Square off the tailstock end, measure 30mm (1 ^{3}/$_{16}$ inch) from that squared off end towards the headstock. At that point part off squarely.

- Hold this centre piece in the chuck with about 3mm (^{1}/$_8$ inch) showing. Before continuing make absolutely sure that the end is flat and square.

- Set a 3mm (^{1}/$_8$ inch) drill into a drill chuck held at the tailstock end. Mark a position 6mm (^{1}/$_4$ inch) away from the drill tip (use typist correction fluid or a small piece of tape).

- Switch on the lathe and drill into the face of the work to the marked depth, then a fraction deeper to ensure a good fit between spigot and drilled hole.

- Withdraw the drill, remove the centre piece from the chuck and reverse it so that the other end may be drilled.

- Drill again to the marked depth plus that fraction. *(Fig. 22.3).*

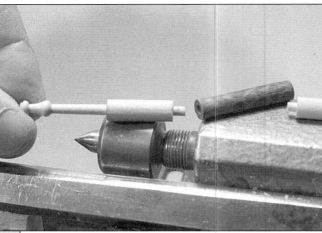

Fig. 22.4. The three parts.

Fig. 22.3. Drilling out the centre.

- If the material held in the chuck is likely to be marked by the chuck jaws either protect the work by wrapping it with a piece of cereal packet or turn the centre piece close to 9mm ($^3/_8$ inch) diameter allowing the bruises caused by the jaws to be turned away later.

- In some cases it is good to make a clear distinction between the centre section and the outer parts. If this is needed then turn two, small, thin collars each with a 3mm ($^1/_8$ inch) hole drilled through. These collars are more effective if they are made from a contrasting colour. They can be slipped onto the spigots between the outer parts and centre piece when they are glued together

- Take the prepared centre and top and tail *(Fig. 22.4)* (and collars if they are to be used). Apply PVA glue to the spigots then fit them into the drilled holes in the centre piece. To cramp them tightly whilst the glue sets hold the head section in the chuck bringing the revolving centre, held in the tailstock, forward to apply pressure to the tail piece.

- When the glue is fully dry treat the whole piece as a normal dowel for bobbin turning. Turn the head and neck first then hold them in the collets turning the body to the desired shape. *(Fig. 22.5).*

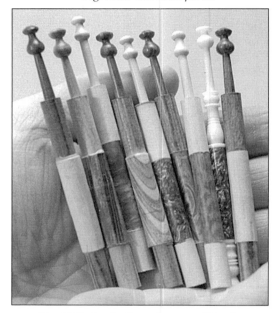

Fig. 22.5. A selection of prepared blanks.

A.   Turu or palmwood.

This provides a most exciting centre for a bobbin but turning this material is like turning a bunch of straws. When turned there are long streaks of deep browns and blacks surrounded by pale brown areas. Sharp tools will produce a good surface. It may be necessary to have collars at either end of this centre part to create the best effect.

B.   Beefwood.

A fine hard Australian wood with an exciting grain. It is beefy brown with a most attractive mottled grain pattern. It does not have sufficient strength when thin to be used to turn satisfactory lace bobbins, this makes

- Take piece one of line one and draw one edge through the glue, then lay it upon the polythene with the glued edge to the right.

- Take piece two of line one and draw one edge through the glue. Lay this second piece with its dry side to the glued side of the first. This leaves the glued side of piece two exposed on the right.

- Take piece three of line one and repeat. Constantly push the pieces together keeping them tight and flat and their tops lined up. *(Fig. 22.20).*

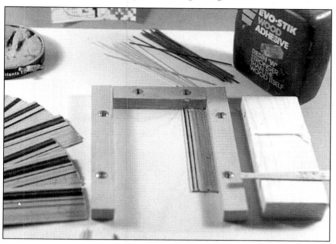

Fig. 22.20. Laying up the lines.

- When all 36 of the first line are in place make sure all are tightly pushed together and that they are flat and that their tops are in line.

- Leave to dry.

- When line one is dry mark a No. 1 on its top right corner, remove it from the polythene and set it to one side.

- Now work on lines 2, 3, 4 & 5 in a similar manner remembering to push them up tightly, to keep them flat and to mark the line number on the top right corner before removing.

- When all five lines are complete and dry carefully clean each surface with a scraper. A Woodworkers' chisel will do. Remember to replace the line number on the top right corner if it is cleaned off.

Gluing The Lines Together.

- Lay line one down on the polythene with No. 1 top right. Glue the top surface.

- Lay line two on top of the glued surface making sure that No. 2 is visible on the top right. Glue the top surface

- Lay line three on top then glue its top surface. *(Fig. 22.21).*

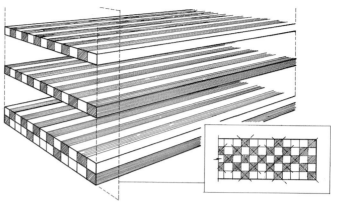

Fig. 22.21. Gluing the lines together.

- Repeat the process with lines 4 & 5. Remember that the final top surface should not be glued and also remember each piece should show its No. at the top right.

> ### *Important*
> *Make sure all lines are accurately aligned in the stack and only then place a piece of polythene on top. Find some heavy weight, a brick maybe, and place it on top to hold the pieces firmly together whilst the glue dries.*

- When the glue has dried take a thin slice from one end to check the pattern.

- If the process has been followed carefully then the pattern should be accurate.

- Set the bandsaw so that a 1mm ($^1/_{24}$ inch) slice may be cut from the block.

- Slice away until sufficient pieces have been cut.

- Again the core size can be calculated.

- Slice width equals 6mm ($^1/_4$ inch). Slice thickness equals 1mm ($^1/_{24}$ inch).

6mm ($^1/_4$ inch) less 1mm ($^1/_{24}$ inch) equals 5mm ($^1/_5$ inch).

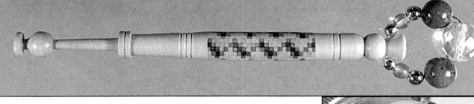

Fig. 22.22. A Tunbridgeware bobbin.

● So cut a 5mm ($^1/_5$ inch) square core from close grained hardwood.

● These slices can be glued to the core in a similar manner to fixing the inlay banding described earlier. Again the pattern arrangement must be considered before the pieces are glued around the core and held in place with elastic bands.

● Finally the fully dried core with the fixed Tunbridgeware can be turned round. *(Fig. 22.23).*

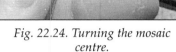

Fig. 22.24. Turning the mosaic centre.

Fig. 22.25. Drilling the mosaic centre.

Fig. 22.23. Starting to turn the mosaic centre.

● Cut a 30mm (1 $^1/_4$ inch) length of the turned core. Hold it in the chuck with only a little showing, square off the end and drill in to accept the spigots turned on the top and tail pieces. *(Fig. 22.24).*

● Reverse the piece in the chuck square off the now exposed end and drill it similarly. *(Fig. 22.25).*

● The diameter of the prepared top and tail must match or be larger than the diameter of the rounded Tunbridgeware centre.

● The Tunbridgeware centre may now be glued between the top and tail pieces and when dry the whole piece may be treated like an ordinary bobbin blank. *(Fig. 22.26).* When turning this blank be particularly careful not to turn through the inlay surface. *(Fig. 22.7).*

Take particular care when turning the Tunbridgeware centres. Tools must be particularly sharp for blunt tools or a deep cut can drag out those small squares of mosaic.

And *PVA glue can be a little rubbery which may allow movement in the mosaic. Although I have had no real problems using this type of glue, if it does not work for you try another type such as Cascamite which is much tougher — but it is more brittle. Whichever glue is used the finished bobbins are worth all the effort.*

Fig. 22.26. Two Tunbridgeware bobbins.

23 – Bitted Bobbins.
(Made in Laburnum).

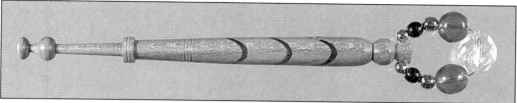

Fig. 23.1. Bitted bobbin.

This is a very descriptive title for this early style of bobbin for these wooden bobbins have "bits" of wood let into their surface in various interesting ways. The two styles of bitted bobbins described here show how saw cuts are filled with veneer which when glued in place can be turned as an integral part of the wood bobbin. The first style involves simple straight saw cuts. The second style has curved saw cuts. Below I will describe how each is made.

For each of these bobbins I begin with a generous 6mm ($^1/_4$ inch) thick blank the usual 95mm (3$^3/_4$ inch) in length.

Starting with the basic bitted bobbin.

● Measure from one end of the blank 15mm ($^5/_8$ inch) up and mark a line around. If the wood is light in colour use a pencil, if it is dark use a white pencil crayon.

● From that point measure 9mm ($^3/_8$ inch) up and mark a second line around.

● From that point measure a further 9mm ($^3/_8$ inch) and mark another line around.

> As the saw cuts will be filled with veneer experimental saw cuts should be made in scrap wood and various thickness of veneer tested for fit. If the saw cut is too wide for a single veneer thickness, added interest can be gained by fitting a sandwich of different coloured veneers.

● To help position the blank in the vice so that the saw cuts may be made, and also to understand the angle at which those cuts are to be made, hold the blank between thumb and forefinger with the pencil marks to the top. Looking down upon the square end consider the top left corner of that end as No.1 and then number 2, 3 and 4 clockwise around. *(Fig. 23.2)*.

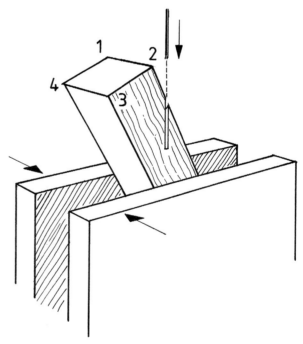

Fig. 23.2. Arranging the blank in the vice.

● Place the blank in the vice at an approximate angle of 45 degrees (top to the left) with the pencil marks uppermost. Take it that corners 3 and 4 are closest. The saw cuts will be made across corner No. 2 of the blank and will go no further than halfway. As the cut is across the corner the half-way mark will be considered to be the imagined diagonal running from corner 1 to corner 3.

Fig. 23.3. Gluing in the veneer.

- Hold the saw so that it is in a natural vertical position. Place the saw on the top pencil mark on corner 2 then keeping contact at that corner move the saw around to the right so that it is set at 45 degrees to the blank. Raise the handle slightly so that a cut may be made at corner 2 to half the thickness (the diagonal between 1 & 3. Fig. 23.2).

- Repeat the cuts at the middle and bottom lines.

- Spread glue upon the pieces of veneer and slip them into the saw cuts. *(Figs. 23.3 & 23.4).*

Fig. 23.4. The veneer fixed in place.

Fig. 23.5. Trimming the veneer.

- Allow the glue to set and using a sharp craft knife carefully trim the veneer flush with the surface of the blank.

- The three remaining cuts may be made on the opposite corner No. 4 in a similar manner described above. Once those cuts have been made they too can have veneer glued in place and once that glue has set those veneer pieces may be trimmed flush.

- The bobbin blank may then be turned as any other but care must be taken when turning the inlaid areas. A heavy cut may break out or dislodge the veneer. *(Fig. 23.6).*

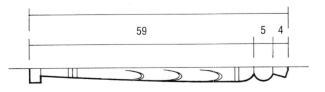

Fig. 23.6. Template.

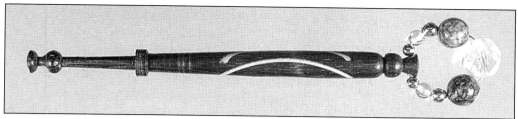

Fig. 23.8. Curved bitted.

Curved Bitted.

(Made in Rosewood). *(Figs. 23.7 & 23.8).*

One of the most intriguing sets of bitted bobbins I have seen were made in the 1830's. A curved trepanning saw (which looks a little like a pastry cutter) was used to run a series of part circular pathways into the wooden blank. Pieces of veneer were then glued into these curved cuts and when dry the piece was turned. One style in particular impressed me, the curved cuts had been made on all four sides of the blank and they were also facing both ways. The one I made in this style was so riddled with saw cuts it fell apart when I began to turn it, yet that 1830's examples (which was glued together with fish glue) has lasted all these years.

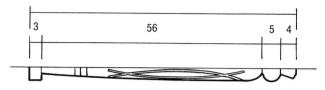

Fig. 23.10. Template.

- The easiest way to prepare this style of bobbin is to use a pillar drill in which has been set a hole cutting saw with a 62mm (2 $^1/_2$ inch) diameter blade in place.

- A simple jig is made to hold the blank in position whilst the hole cutting saw is brought down onto the work. The jig is described below. *(Figs. 23.9 & 23.11).*

- First of all arrange the pillar drill table so that it sits centrally.

- Take a piece of 9mm ($^3/_8$ inch) ply about 25mm (1 inch) wider all round than the size of the drill table.

- Place the ply centrally upon the drill table so that 25mm (1 inch) overhangs each edge.

- Using a pencil carefully mark on the underside of the ply around the edge of the drill table.

- Lift the ply off, turn it over then pin and glue 9mm ($^3/_8$ inch) square pieces of pine to the outer edge of those pencil lines. Replace it on the drill table adjusting the small blocks until it fits snugly.

Fig. 23.7. A variety of bitted bobbins.

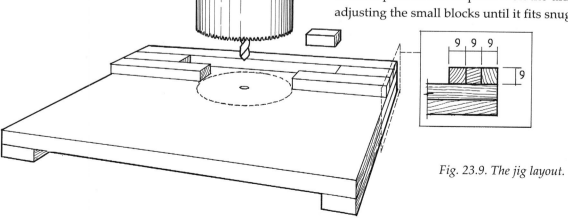

Fig. 23.9. The jig layout.

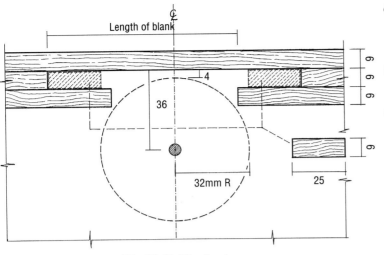

Fig. 23.11. The jig sizes.

- Bring the hole cutting saw down and drill into the ply producing a locating hole.

- Switch off the drill then draw a pencil line from the centre of the drilled hole towards the pillar.

- From the centre of the drilled hole towards the pillar measure 35mm (1 $^3/_8$ inch) along the pencil line. At that point mark a full line across, parallel to the back edge of the ply and also at 90 degrees to that first pencil line.

- Pin and glue a length of 9mm ($^3/_8$ inch) square pine on the pillar side of that line.

Fig. 23.12. The blank in place and a finished blank.

- Measure 9mm ($^3/_8$ inch) from that block towards the centre marking a second line parallel to the first.

- Pin and glue a length of 9mm ($^3/_8$ inch) square pine on the centre side of that line.

- Next measure 60mm (just under 2 $^1/_2$ inch) from the first pencil line to the right and then to the left along the channel between the two fixed pieces of 9mm ($^3/_8$ inch) wood. Mark those positions carefully. On the outer edges of those two marked lines glue in a small length of 9mm ($^3/_8$ inch) square pine. This will leave an open gap of about 120mm (4 $^3/_4$ inch) long.

- Cut a piece of 9mm ($^3/_8$ inch) square wood to an exact 25mm (1 inch) length as a filler block. Turn a small piece of 3mm ($^1/_8$ inch) dowel and fit it into the top edge of this piece to act as a simple handle.

- The jig is complete, a 95mm (3 $^3/_4$ inch) long 9mm ($^3/_8$ inch) square blank of the chosen wood can be fitted into the gap then the filler block can be pushed to one end or the other to lock the blank firmly in place.(Fig.23.12).

Cutting The Grooves.

With the blank in place the drill is switched on and the hole saw is brought down and a cut is made into the blank's surface. Set the depth stop so that the blade cuts to about 4mm (1/6 inch) deep. The curved cut is filled with veneer which has had glue applied to its surface. The piece is set on one side until the glue has dried, the veneer may then be trimmed level with the blank's surface using a sharp craft knife. The blank can then be repositioned in the jig with the next clean face uppermost ready for the hole cutting saw to cut a curved pathway. The curved cut can again be filled with glued veneer, trimmed and repositioned. The blank is worked in this manner until the desired set of veneer filled curved cuts have been produced.

The jig has been designed so that these curved cuts can be made in either direction and on all four sides. (Fig. 23.14)

Fig. 23.14. Turned and polished.

When these curved bitted blanks have been satisfactorily produced, all the veneer glued and trimmed, the blank can be turned like any other blank. Remember to turn carefully around the veneer areas for some pieces may be torn out if the tools are not kept sharp. *(Fig. 23.13)*. Also remember that the laminated area may be a little weaker than the solid wood around it. *(Template Fig. 23.10)*.

Fig. 23.13. Turning the blank.

In most cases the curved cut will have to be filled with veneer which is glued in place, left to dry, then trimmed before it is replaced for another cut. The technique described above is best suited for a production run. Prepare 10 to 20 blanks, make the first curved cut in each, glue the veneer in place then trim. Make the second cut in each blank, glue the veneer, trim etc.. The veneer pieces need to be cut 6mm ($^1/_4$ inch) wide by 45mm (1 $^3/_4$ inch) long.

It will be seen that by lifting the filler block and moving it to the opposite end, when the blank is replaced (making sure that it is also turned top to tail), the curved cut made will be opposite that of the first. If the cut is made on the same surface as the first they will cross.

By lifting and turning the blank an interested effect can be achieved which is quite different to that produced if the blank remains at one end of the jig only. When the hole saw is cutting the curved pathway the blank needs to be held firmly in place.

Fig. 23.15. Cross curved bitted.

To ensure that the jig can be replaced accurately each time turn a small piece of wood 25mm (1 inch) long. 12mm ($^1/_2$ inch) of which is turned to 25mm (1 inch) diameter the remaining part is turned to fit the hole in the centre of the drill table. Remove the jig which at the moment is accurately located. Fit the turned plug into the hole in the drill table. Switch on the drill and bring the hole saw down so that the central 6mm ($^1/_4$ inch) drill, drills into that plug. Switch off the drill allowing hole cutting saw to be lifted away. If the pillar drill table is moved between the times the jig is used it can easily be relocated. Just fit the turned plug into the hole in the pillar drill table re-align the drill bit with the hole in the top of the plug and then you will be sure that the jig may be replaced accurately. *(Figs. 23.16 & 23.17).*

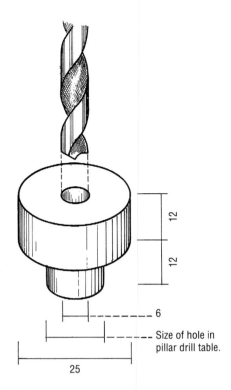

Fig. 23.17. Sizes for the location plug.

Fig. 23.16. The locator.

Fig. 23.18. Cross curved bitted turned.

24 – Mother And Babe.
(Made in Yew.)

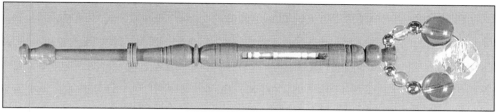

Fig. 24.1. Mother and babe.

Lacemaking folklore suggests that it is unlucky for an unmarried lacemaker to have a Mother and Babe bobbin on her lace pillow. The consequence, no doubt, would be to bear an illegitimate child but what about an unmarried turner turning this style of bobbin?

It may seem strange to begin a Mother and Babe bobbin by first turning the babe but it is a more efficient method of work. If more than one of this type of bobbin is to be turned then turn a batch of babes first.

> *When turning baby bobbins I always choose a contrasting coloured wood for the babe so that it is more easily seen but more important than the choice of wood is the quality of the turning. Even though this bobbin is small and partly hidden inside the "mother" it must be as good as, if not better than, the main bobbin.*

Turning the baby bobbin.

● Set the 6mm (1/4 inch) diameter piece of wood in the chuck with about 32mm (1 1/4 inch) showing. Bring the tailstock holding the revolving centre forward to support the end.

● When turning these smaller bobbins I use smaller tools. A small square end and skew are an advantage but a 9mm ($^3/_8$ inch) gouge is fine. It is not absolutely necessary to use smaller tools but it does make the work a little easier.

● Use the gouge to clean down to just under 3mm ($^1/_8$ inch) so that the finished baby bobbin will slide easily into the, soon to be, drilled out centre of the mother bobbin.

> *The template for this small piece is a previously turned babe supaglued to the end of a piece of perspex. It is far easier to see and to handle than a tiny piece of card. Drill a hole in the perspex and it may be hung up. (Mark out from Fig.24.7).*

● Bring the template to the rotating work and mark in pencil the major positions. *(Figs. 24.2 & 24.3).*

● Use the square end tool to slice/shape the tail and to cut into the body at the collar.

Fig. 24.2. Template the difficult way.

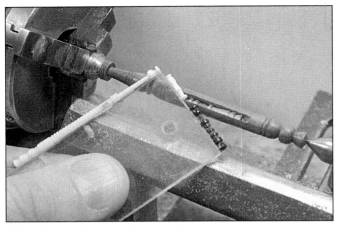

Fig. 24.3. Template fixed on perspex.

- Next take the skew chisel and clean off the end of the tail then round the bulb next to the tail. The skew can be used to turn the area down from the bulb to the collar.

- Use the corner of the square end tool to mark a series of incised lines upon the body of the bobbin. This provides a little texture to the surface. The square end tool can then be used to cut down to the neck cutting cleanly to around 1.5mm ($^1/_{16}$ inch.) diameter.

Fig. 24.5. Finishing the babe.

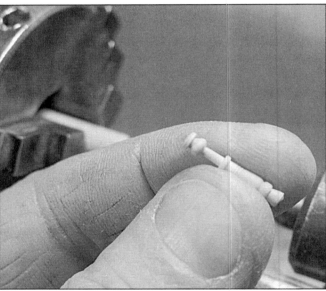

Fig. 24.6. The baby bobbin.

- Bring the skew and begin to shape the head using the same movements when turning a full sized bobbin.

- Lightly glass-paper the finished babe then polish. Finally part off at the tail end using the small skew.

Fig. 24.4. Turning the babe.

Turning The "Mother" Bobbin. *(Template Fig.24.7)*

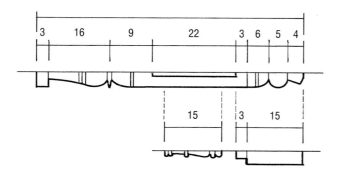

Fig. 24.7. Template.

- The blank length for this style of bobbin needs to be greater than that needed for the basic bobbin. Account needs to be taken of the turned plug which will fit into the drilled out hollow.

- Begin with a piece 3mm ($^1/_8$ inch) longer than normal.

- Turn the head and neck the usual size and shape.

- Hold the blank, with the turned head and neck deep in the chuck, so that about 32mm ($^1/_4$ inch) length is showing and is supported by the tailstock.

- Measure 15mm ($^5/_8$ inch) from the tailstock and mark in pencil.

- From that point measure a further 3mm ($^1/_8$ inch) and mark again.

- Turn that small section between the two marks down to 3mm ($^1/_8$ inch) diameter using a square end tool. If this tool is twisted slightly anti-clockwise and moved to the left it will take a slicing cut. Similarly if twisted slightly clockwise and moved to the right the same slicing cut will be made. This will cause, what most seem to think of as a scraping tool to cut.

- The internal corners of this section can be cleaned out using the corner of the square end tool.

- Check the size of the plug regularly against the drill chosen to hollow the mother bobbin. *(Fig. 24.8).*

Fig. 24.8. Measuring the plug.

- Once the plug has been turned to shape mark a pencil datum line across the main body and the end of the plug.

- Cut the plug away from the main body on the headstock side leaving the 3mm ($^1/_8$ inch) turned section joined to the tailstock side.

- Set the plug aside.

- Loosen the chuck then slide the main body inwards until a few millimetres (a fraction of an inch) is left exposed. Tighten the chuck.

- Square off the face of the blank.

> *It is important to drill precisely on centre so prepare the end of the blank by turning a small hollow using the corner of the square end tool. Do not force the drill into the blank too quickly for this may cause the drill to run off centre. Regularly withdraw the drill to clean out shavings this will prevent overheating of both blank and drill bit.*

- Into a drill chuck fit a 3mm ($^1/_8$ inch) drill and fit the chuck to the tailstock.

- Mark a point on the drill body 25mm (1 inch) away from the cutting point. A small piece of tape, typist correction fluid or a drilled out wood sleeve (which I prefer) can be used to gauge the depth to which the drill should cut.

- Move the tool rest aside bringing the tailstock, drill and chuck forward.

- Drill into the body of the bobbin until the depth mark is reached. Withdraw The drill regularly to prevent overheating and cracking of the blank. (Fig. 24.9).

Fig. 24.9. Drilling into the "mother".

- Remove the blank from the chuck then fit the plug into the drilled hole aligning the datum marks. If the plug does not fit use a needle file to remove some wood until a satisfactory fit is achieved.

- Take the brass collets and fit them around the head and neck then hold in the chuck. Bring the revolving centre forward to support the end. It should run on centre as the plug was centred when turned.

- The bobbin blank can now the treated as any other blank.

- Mark in pencil upon the rotating blank the major positions using the template as a guide. (Fig. 24.10).

- Use the square end tool to slice cut the tail and the area below the collar close to the chuck.

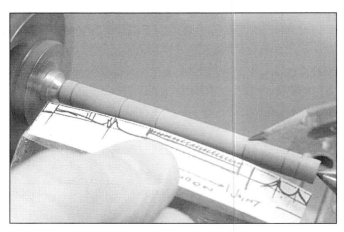

Fig. 24.10. Marking out the bobbin.

- Next use the skew to face off the end of the tail and to turn the bulb.

- Turn the thin collar and bulb at the headstock side of the centre and make a series of sweeping cuts from that bulb to the collar.

- Use the square end tool to mark incised lines on the collar, the body as decoration, and at the start and finish points of the window openings. These last two cuts need to be made lightly so as not to cut into the hollow beneath which would weaken this area. These "start" and "finish" incised lines help prevent the window cuts from chipping out.

- Choose one chuck jaw to act as an index.

- Bring it to 12 o'clock.

Fig. 24.11. Dremel 199 cutter.

- Into the Pendant drill fit a Dremel No. 199 tool. *(Fig 24.11)*. (No. 199 is like a small, thick, circular saw on the end of a shaft.) If this tool is not available in your area take a suitably sized and shaped pan headed nail and carefully, if not tediously, file a series of teeth around the edge of the head. Use a triangular needle file and make sure that the teeth are filed so that they face the correct way so that when rotating they will cut. This nail can then be used in the same way as the 199 to cut the windows in the bobbin.

- Now cautiously, with the tool rotating, bring it to the top of the work between the two incised lines.

- Keep the tool close to the headstock incised line then push the rotating tool down into the work allowing it to cut into the wood easily. *(Fig. 24.12)*.

Fig. 24.13. Finishing the cut.

Fig. 24.12. Cutting the window.

- Make sure that it cuts up to the headstock incised line then carefully move it towards the tailstock until it reaches the second incised line.

- Keep the tool, when cutting this window, parallel to be body.

- Halt when it reaches the line then remove it. *(Fig.24.13)*.

Take care when using this tool. Keep both hands behind the direction of the cutting edge. Be cautious. Do not force the tool, allow it to cut easily. Practice on sample pieces until satisfied that a straight and SAFE cut may be made.

Other methods include using a small router with a guide, which fits on the lathe, allowing windows to be cut in a more controlled manner, or using a drill to start and finish the window, the area between the drilled holes can then be sawn or filed away.

I have chosen the method illustrated here for it is more direct, it is hand work requiring skill which I find more satisfying.

- When the first window has been cut move the chuck index jaw to 3 o'clock and repeat.

- When the second window has been cut move the index jaw to 6 o'clock, cut the third window, then finally move the index jaw to 9 o'clock to complete the fourth window.

- Clean up each of the windows using a needle file. Check the datum mark across the plug and body of the bobbin.

- Withdraw the tailstock and the plug from the bobbin.

- Slide the baby bobbin fully into the hollow making sure that it is the correct way round, head of the babe towards the headstock. *(Fig. 24.14).*

Fig. 24.15. The finished bobbin.

Fig. 24.14. Fitting the babe.

The Mother and Babe bobbin described here is a simple form. With imagination many various styles can be produced. It is not necessary for a baby bobbin to be fitted inside, other items such as tiny beads, seeds, tinsel or whatever takes your fancy can fill the centre of the mother bobbin.

- Apply glue, PVA is my choice, to the plug and re-fit aligning the datum marks. Bring the tailstock up to add pressure whilst the glue dries.

- When the glue has fully dried switch on the lathe and turn away any excess glue from around the joint.

- Use the corner of the square end tool to cut an incised line into the joint and one either side to disguise that joint.

- Lightly glasspaper then polish the bobbin. *(Fig. 24.15).*

25 – Hinge Spangle.
(Made in laburnum).

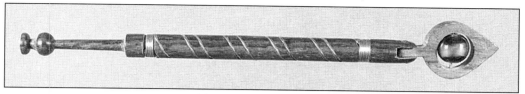

Fig. 25.1. Hinge spangle.

Although the hinge spangle is not the most efficient form of spangle it is the most decorative. In the 19th century the hinge spangle took various forms, a three lobed shape with a bead in each lobe, the more common inverted teardrop and also diamond shape.

Once the basic technique of making these hinge spangles is understood any shape may be cut and fitted to the base of a bobbin, but consideration must be given to the tail shape of that bobbin to accommodate the hinge slot and retain strength.

- Select a piece of wood which matches the bobbin.

- From that piece prepare a 25mm (inch) square which is 3mm ($^1/_8$ inch) thick.

- Choose a hinge shape from the drawings and then mark that shape upon the prepared piece of wood. *(Figs.25.2 & 25.5)*.

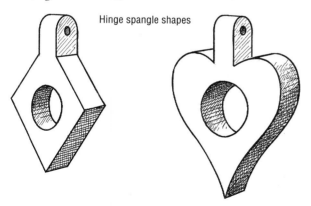

Hinge spangle shapes

Fig. 25.2. Diamond and heart shapes.

- Measure the bead (or beads) diameter which will fit in the hinge shape, add 2mm ($1^1/_{12}$ inch) to that measurement and select a drill of that size (or as close as possible.)

- Stick a piece of masking tape to the back of the wood to prevent it from splitting out.

- Drill through the shape at the marked points being particularly careful when the drill cuts through as too much force, or a blunt drill may split the wood. *(Fig. 25.3)*.

Fig. 25.3. Drilling the holes.

- Once all the holes have been drilled, cut around the shape using a fret saw. *(Fig. 25.4)*.

- Clean the outside of the hinge shape and around the drilled holes. Use needle files and fine glass-paper until satisfied that all edges are well finished.

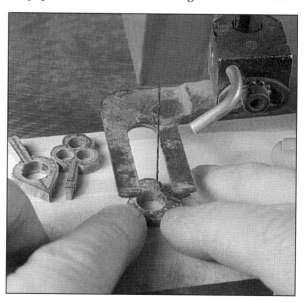

Fig. 25.4. Cutting the shape.

- Round over the top part of the hinge to allow it to swing freely in the tail slot — see diagram. *(Fig. 25.5).*

Fig. 25.5. Fitting to the bobbin.

- When the shaping is complete polish the piece to a finish which matches the bobbin.

- The beads are held in the hinge upon brass pins. Judge carefully exactly where holes should be drilled in the side of the hinge shape so that a brass lace pin may be pushed through to support the bead. When this has been done and the beads are held in place carefully supaglue the ends of the pin. Clip off close and file the end smooth.

- Next cut the slot in the bobbin tail to accept the top part of the hinge. *(Fig. 25.6)* This is a little over 3mm ($^1/_8$ inch) and about 6mm ($^1/_4$ inch) long. The hinge will be fixed upon a brass pin through the bobbin tail.

Fig. 25.6. Cutting the slot in the tail.

- Carefully decide exactly where the hole for this brass pivot pin needs to be drilled. Holding the hinge in the tail slot drill through bobbin and hinge.

- Fit the brass pivot pin through tail and hinge then very carefully supaglue it in place making sure that it is only glued at either side of the bobbin. The hinge must be free to move. Clip off excess pin and using a needle file clean it back smoothly.

- If you have been successful in producing these hinge spangles in wood try producing some in bone.

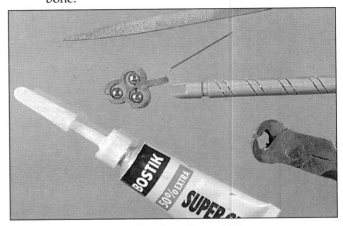

Fig. 25.7. File, pins, glue and clippers.

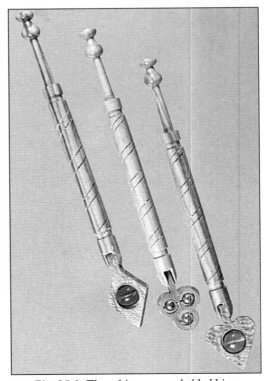

Fig. 25.8. Three hinge spangled bobbins.

Part 3
Bone Bobbins

Turning bone blank round.

This is delicate work and to begin with bone may seem to be very brittle. Light fine cuts are best. Become familiar with the material before rushing at it hard and heavy handed. Only your experience will allow you to judge how much pressure must be applied when cutting.

Both the squared end and round nose tools will cut shavings, they do not scrape. Learn to "find the cut" of the tool then let it run along the work.

Bone can be shaped to produce very sharp edges. Do not produce sharp edges on the head for they will cut threads. Also those sharp edges can cut fingers so do not run your finger on the rotating work to check the finish.

Don't become despondent if breakages occur. I used to break quite a number of bone bobbins, but I very rarely break them now, so just keep at it. Keep the broken pieces for when you become more proficient you will be able to make a variety of items from them.

Remember to keep your tools extremely sharp for bone is not very forgiving. Most breakages are caused by blunt tools.

26 – Turning Bone Bobbins.

Turning bone

Turning bone is a most pleasant experience for the finest details and crispiest edges can be achieved. It is a material which shows, to greater effect, decoration applied to its surface.

The tools I use to turn bone are quite simple. The square end tool and the skew chisel which were used to turn wood work extremely well on bone. To rough down and remove larger amounts then a round nose tool ground from a cheap 6mm ($^1/_4$ inch) wood chisel is the ideal tool. *(Fig.26.1).*

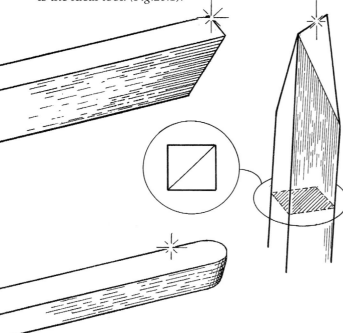

Fig. 26.1. Round nose, square end and skew chisel.

Rounding Bone

- Cut the blank to the usual bobbin length, 95mm (3 $^3/_4$ inch). If a Mother and Babe bobbin is to be made then the blank length needs to be 100mm (4 inch).

- Hold the end of the square blank in the chuck and support the other end with a revolving centre.

- Take the round nose tool, switch the lathe on, move the tool gently towards the rotating blank.

- Very light cuts must be taken at the start. Only a small section close to the tailstock, about 9mm ($^3/_8$ inch) in length, should be turned fully round. It will be noticed that the round nose tool, when it cuts into fully round bone, actually cuts shavings from the bone.

- Switch the lathe off and reverse the blank holding the now rounded section firmly in the chuck. Support the tail end with the revolving centre.

- Now the rest of the bone blank may be fully rounded. Begin with light cuts but as the bone comes closer to round then slightly heavier cuts may be taken.

- If you have not turned bone before you will notice the tough nature of this material. You may also notice how brittle it can be at times. If you experience problems turning bone then consider other problems you have encountered when turning and remember how they were overcome. With a little time and effort the technique will be mastered. Experience conquers most problems.

The odd shaped blank may be difficult to hold in the chuck. It is important that one end is held firmly whilst the other end is rounded.

Some bone blanks may be a little bent. The best way to round these, so that the maximum diameter is achieved, is to offset the blank at the tail end making the centre part of the blank run true (or as close as possible) .The tail end can then be turned round and when that is held in the chuck the whole blank will run more truly allowing the largest possible diameter to be turned.

27 – Bone Heads & Necks.

The bone head and neck is turned in a similar manner to the wooden head and neck but there are a couple of changes. The first is that the gouge is replaced with a round nose tool, and this is used to remove larger quantities of material. The second is that the shaping of the head is a little different from that produced in wood for as bone is more dense it does not need to be buttressed and the top therefore can be turned straighter and thinner.

- Fit the rounded piece of bone into the chuck leaving about 40mm (1 $^5/_8$ inch) exposed.

- Bring the revolving centre up and centre it upon the end of the bone piece. Carefully apply pressure. Judgment needs to be used here for overtightening can cause the bone to split during turning. Only tighten with sufficient strength to support the end.

- Use the round nose tool to bring the outer surface smooth. Remove as little material as possible.

- Take the template and transfer the marks to the revolving blank using a pencil. Line up the head end of the template to the tailstock end of the bone piece. *(Figs 27.1 & 27.2).*

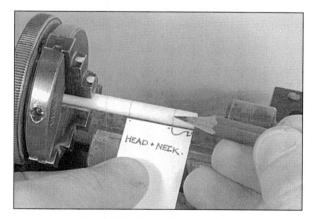

Fig. 27.1. Using the template.

- Using a square end tool cut into the bone piece at the pencil marked shoulder widening the cut to prevent the tool from being gripped. Turn down to about 3mm ($^1/_8$ inch). *(Fig. 27.3).*

When using the square end tool to cut a groove into bone it is best to be a little nervous for that slight shake of the hand causes the cut groove to be wider than the tool and this will prevent it from being gripped and drawn into the work.

```
15      10
|—————|———|
```

Fig. 27.2. Template.

Fig. 27.3. Using the square end tool.

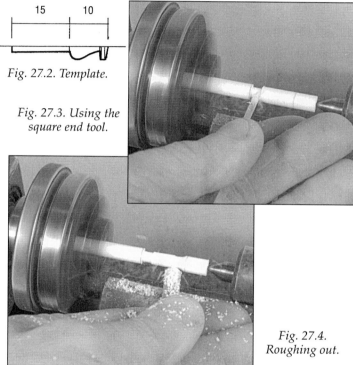

Fig. 27.4. Roughing out.

- Take the round nose tool and rough out the neck area from the head to the shoulder. Many light cuts are better than one heavy cut. *(Fig. 27.4).*

- Turn down close to 3mm ($^1/_8$ inch) diameter.

- Use the skew chisel to shape the top of the head down to the revolving centre. *(Fig. 27.5).*

- Leave about 2mm ($^1/_{12}$ inch) then using the skew slice down to begin the small neck.

- Move the skew slightly so that the cut can come from the left into that slice cut. Work both cuts (Slice down, then cut from the left, both joining) until the area for the small neck has been excavated. *(Fig.27.6).*

Fig. 27.5.
Trimming the top.

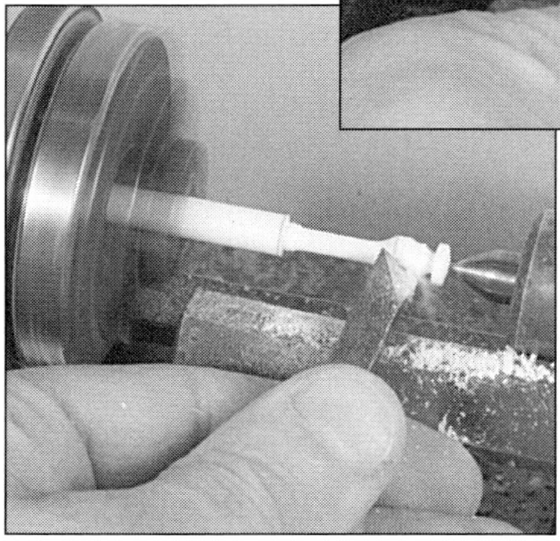

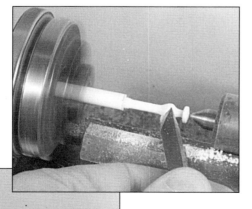

Fig. 27.6.
Turning the small neck.

- Move to the bulb and work down into the small neck. The motion begins as a slice but becomes more of a rolling cut to produce that fluent curve from the bulb to the small neck.

- Next work the bulb fluently over the opposite way (from right over and down to left) to meet the neck. Make sure that the bulb is smoothly shaped. It is also most important that the edges of the rim, at the top of the head, are not sharp for sharp edges will cut lace thread. *(Fig. 27.7).*

Fig. 27.7.
Shaping the bulb.

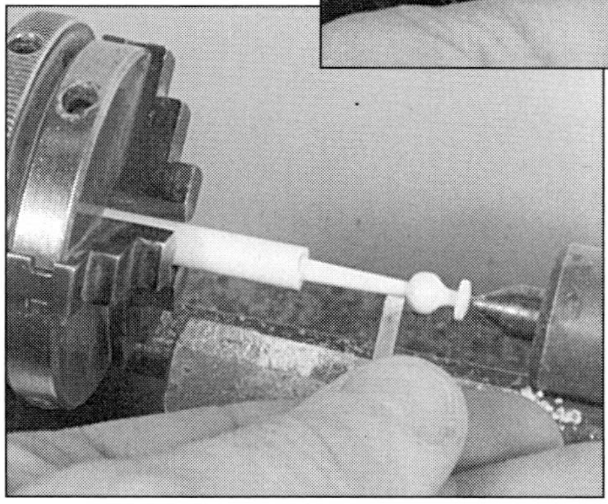

Fig. 27.8.
Cleaning the neck.

- Take the square end tool and use it to clean the neck down to 3mm ($^1/_8$ inch) diameter. Make the shoulder end slightly larger so that it tapers towards the head this will make it look far more balanced. *(Fig 27.8).*

- Again when using the square end tool twist it slightly anti-clockwise then move it along the work to the left. It will be noticed that the tool will cut like a skew chisel producing a clean crisp finish. If the tool is twisted slightly clockwise and moved to the right it will take a planing cut like a miniature skew. Clean in the corners of the shoulder and close to the bulb using the corner of the square end tool. *(Figs 27.9 & 27.10).*

Fig. 27.9.
The square end...

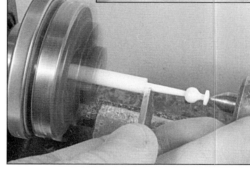

Fig. 27.10.
...cleaning the neck.

- Glass-paper lightly but do not rub out the fine detail. *(Fig. 27.11).*

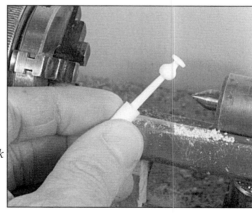

Fig. 27.11.
Head and neck complete.

28 – Decorative Bone Bobbin.

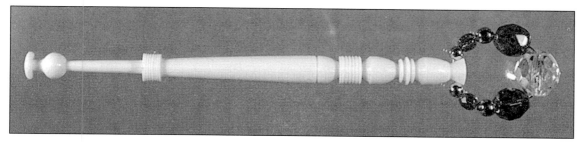

Fig. 28.1. Decorative bone bobbin.

I enjoy turning bone for it takes an edge very well, producing crisp, clean decoration. It is worth working at the techniques to attain that crispness of turning for it shows quality and skill.

The decoratively turned bobbin shown here may appear to be a difficult piece of turning but taken in its parts it is quite simple.

● Take the prepared blank holding the head and neck in the brass collets which can then be held in the chuck. Bring the centre up to support the end making sure that it is centred accurately.

● Switch on the lathe and using a round nose tool to turn the piece so that it is fully round and any "throw" is turned out. Remove as little material as possible keeping the blank as close to 6mm ($1/4$ inch) diameter.

● Use the card template to transfer the major points to the rotating blank using a pencil. *(Fig.28.2).*

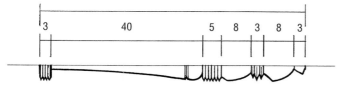

Fig. 28.2. Template.

● Take the square end tool and gently shape the tail then turn a small groove below the collar, at the head end, about 4mm ($1/6$ inch) diameter. *(Fig. 28.3).*

● Set aside the square end tool and use the round nose tool to cut a slope from the start of the decorative area down towards the collar into that turned groove.

● Next use the skew chisel to produce a cut which will round over into the start of the decoration at A. *(Fig.28.4).* This is done by angling the skew to

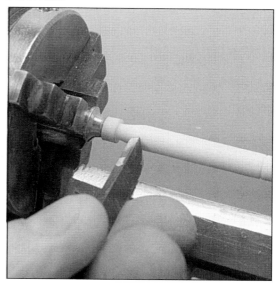

Fig. 28.3. Cutting into the collar.

the right and cutting a small notch at A., then working into that notch rolling the skew to cut the curve and also to cut more deeply. The skew may be twisted more fully to the right so that its edge is close to upright. The lower corner may be used to square up the flat face abutting the curve which has just been cut. When satisfied use the skew to slice the end of the tail down to the centre to finish the end neatly.

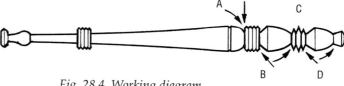

Fig. 28.4. Working diagram.

● Now work at the squared shoulder B, this time twisting the skew to the left to cut an initial notch. Slice down into that notch to produce a small angled face. The square shoulder may be trimmed by twisting the skew further to the left until the edge is almost upright then the lower corner may be used to make a slicing cut.

- From the top of the small angled face which has been cut at B begin to turn down towards C using the skew. The skew should be twisted slightly to the right and a notch cut at C first. The cut can then progress rounding over and down with a light slicing action. Stop when satisfied and do not "fiddle", cut directly and decisively.

- Leave the decorative area at C and work the angled face from D down towards C. *(Fig. 28.5).* Again twist the skew slightly to the left and cut a notch at C, then slice down into it to produce that angled face.

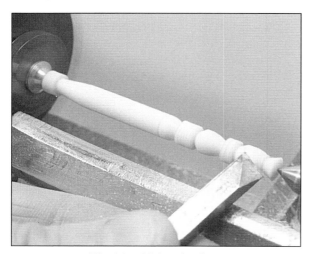

Fig. 28.5. Using the skew.

- Next round over from the top of the angled face at D to the angled tail. Twist the skew slightly to the right then with rolling, slicing cuts shape the area down to the tail. *(Fig. 28.6).*

- Now for the decoration at C. In your mind divide that area into three. The centre piece will be left standing proud. Working on the left of centre, with the skew slightly twisted to the right, cut into that area reducing its diameter to about 4mm ($^1/_6$ inch). Next twist the skew more to the right until it is almost upright then slice between the two parts. Pull the skew back and twist it to the left until the edge is almost upright then slice the edge of the centre piece down into that cut. This angles the centre piece slightly. Move to the left and slice, at the same angle, the outer edge of C down to B.

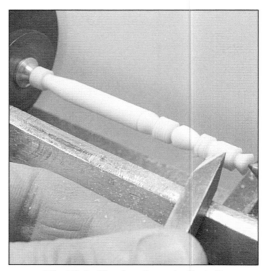

Fig. 28.6. Shaping down to the tail.

- Still at C, now move to the right of that centre piece and cut the right hand third down to 4mm ($^1/_6$ inch) diameter. Twist the skew to the left until the blade is almost upright and slice down between the two parts. Twist the skew to the right so that the edge is almost upright and take an angled slice on the centre piece down into the cut between the two parts. This will complete the shaping on the centre part.

- Now move to the right hand outside edge of C and slice down to D with the skew at the same angle.

- Set aside the skew taking up the square end tool.

- Now use the corner of the square end tool to cut lines on the broad area which is left between A & B.

- Cut a series of lines on the collar and cut three below the shaped bulb at A.

- To finish, glass-paper just enough to make the bobbin comfortable to handle but not so that all those crisp features are rounded off.

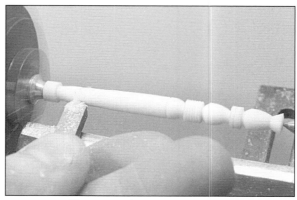

Fig. 28.7. Cleaning up the body.

29 – Candy Wired.

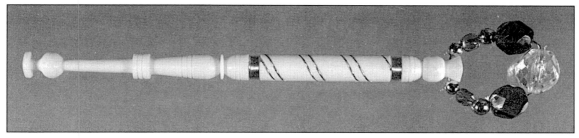

Fig. 29.1. Candy wired.

This is a simply made but effective bone bobbin. A parallel pair of wire spirals snake around the bobbin body. There is something most satisfying about those two tramlines of wire, a naturally easy form.

● With the head and neck held in the collets in the chuck, carefully turn the body evenly round using the round nose tool.

● Whilst the lathe is running transfer the marks from the template to the bobbin blank using a pencil. Carefully mark the tail, the wire grooves, the small collar next to the top wire groove and the collar close to the collets. *(Fig.29.2).*

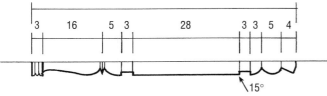

Fig. 29.2. Template.

● Use the square end tool to cut under the collar, next to the collets, down to about 4mm ($1/6$ inch) diameter.

● Next move to the wire grooves cutting those to a similar depth. *(Fig. 29.3).*

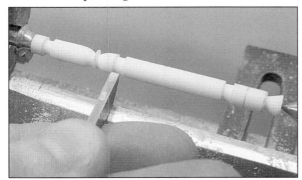

Fig. 29.3. Cutting the wire grooves.

● Still using the square end tool slice down with a series of small cuts to produce the angled tail.

● Set aside the square end tool and take up the skew. Turn off the end of the tail down to the revolving centre then turn the bulb next to the tail.

● To turn the bulb start at top dead centre. Twist the skew slightly to the right and use a rolling slicing action to make a series of cuts down towards the tail to produce the right hand side of the bulb. *(Fig. 29.4).*

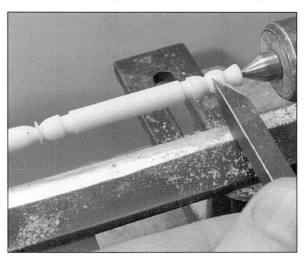

Fig. 29.4. Turning the bulb.

● Judge by eye the distance from top dead centre to the point where the bulb should finish on the left. At that point use the skew, still slightly twisted to the right, to make a cut which marks that position. *(Fig. 29.5).*

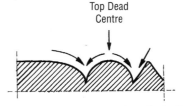

Fig. 29.5. Diagram, turning the bulb.

- Now replace the skew at top dead centre twisting it slightly to the left. Again use a rolling, slicing action cut down into that marked position to produce the left hand side of the bulb. (Fig. 29.6).

Fig. 29.6. The cut.

- A final light cut either side of the bulb may be needed to "neaten" it up.

- Now cut the curved shoulder from the wire groove down to the bulb. This technique is much the same as cutting the right hand side of the bulb.

- When that has been turned move to the small collar close to the top wire groove A similar technique is used to shape the curved shoulder from the wire groove down to the left and also the curved shoulder opposing it, but that of course is turned down to the right. Two half bulbs, which are facing each other, have now been turned with a thin "collar" left between them. This piece can then be sliced down at an angle on either side to produce a nicely shaped collar.

- Now take the round nose tool and turn down from that last curved shoulder into the groove close to the chuck. Finish the sweeping curve using the skew. It will be noticed that both the skew and the round nose tool produce shavings.

- Lay down the skew chisel and take up the square end tool. Use its corner to make two lines on the collar close to the chuck, three lines on the curved shoulder and two lines to the right of the right hand wire groove and the left of the left hand wire groove (see template).

- Switch off the lathe.

- Cutting the wire spirals is exactly the same as described in the section on wooden bobbins.

- The junior hacksaw should have its blade set in backwards to prevent "grab". The saw is gently moved backwards and forwards whilst the left hand slowly rotates the chuck anti-clockwise. At first this method may seem awkward but after a short time it becomes extremely easy. (Fig. 29.7).

- The second wire groove is cut parallel to the first in the exactly the same way but it is set about 3mm ($^1/_8$ inch) away. Use your eye to judge the progress of the saw as it cuts ensuring that it remains parallel.

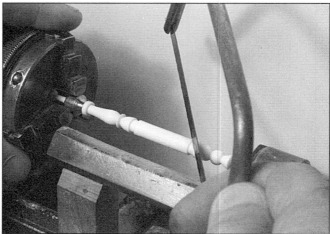

Fig. 29.7. Cutting the wire spirals.

It is important to keep the saw blade at the chosen angle and also upright. Do not twist it for it can chip out the bone around the cut. If the bone does begin to chip around the saw cut, first check whether the blade is blunt. If it is, replace with a sharp blade. If the blade is sharp then the most likely cause is twisting so work carefully. Do not be too dismayed this time if you have produced a ragged cut for it can be disguised. Use a flat fissure burr in the pendant drill and run it up the saw cuts making it into a candy fairing bone bobbin (a bobbin with two parallel twists which are filled with coloured tinsel.)

30 – Bone Caterpillar.

Fig. 30.1. Caterpillar.

A most descriptive name for this bobbin whose decoration creeps lumpily up the body. Each small segment may be decorated with a drilled dot or left plain as one chooses.

- The blank is held in the chuck as before with the head and neck held in collets and the revolving centre supporting the tail end exactly on centre.

- Having turned the blank to ensure that it is smooth and running truly on centre mark out, in pencil, the important points using the template as a guide. *(Fig.30.2).*

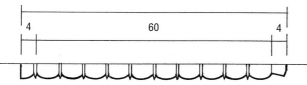

| 4 | 60 | 4 |

Fig. 30.2 template.

\# Turn the tail using square end tool *(Fig. 30.3)* then begin turning each segment. *(Fig. 30.4)* Now this may be done in one of two ways.

Fig. 30.3. Turning the tail and making a start.

1. Either turn the right hand curve of the segment nearest the tail then the left hand curve completing it before moving to the next segment.

Or 2. Turn all the right hand curves of each then all the left hand curves.

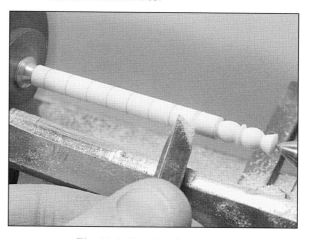

Fig. 30.4. Cutting the "start".

Whichever method is chosen the technique is the same as, follows.

- Hold the skew set at top dead centre of the first segment slightly twisted to the right. *(Fig. 30.5).*

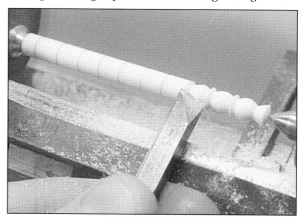

Fig. 30.5. Cutting to the right.

- Use a rolling, slicing cut to shape the right hand half down to the tail. (All other right hand halves may be turned in this manner.)

- To cut the left hand side of the bulb hold the skew slightly twisted to the left. Mark the position of the valley between the segments and using a rolling, slicing cut work from the top dead centre of that segment down into that valley. A thin collar may be left in the valley neatly dividing each segment. (All other left hand halves may be turned in this manner.) *(Fig. 30.6).*

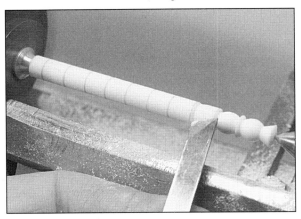

Fig. 30.6. Cutting to the left.

- To drill the dots on the top of each segment choose one jaw of the chuck as an index. *(Fig. 30.7).*

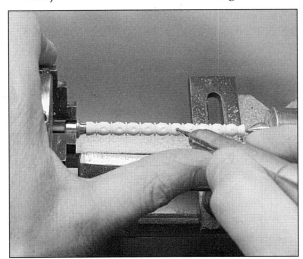

Fig. 30.7. Drilling the dots.

- Bring it to 12 o'clock and mark a pencil line across the top of all the segments.

- Move the jaw to 3 o'clock, 6 o'clock and 9 o'clock in turn, and at each position mark a pencil line across the top of the segments.

- On top of each segment, on the pencil line, use a round burr held in the pendant drill to drill a neat round hole.

When drilling the dot make sure that the burr is rotating quite quickly before pushing it into the bone otherwise the burr may skid off the marked position.

- When all the dots have been drilled paint them in. I use an Acrylic paint and carefully fill in the drilled dots using an extremely fine paint brush. It is worth the time spent applying the paint carefully for any misdirected brush strokes have to be cleaned off. *(Fig. 30.8).*

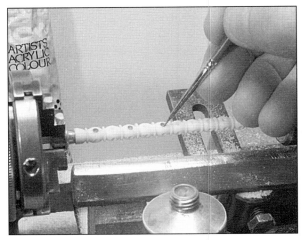

Fig. 30.8. Painting the dots.

- Once the paint is dry use a fine file to remove any excess paint then clean the whole bobbin with a light touch of glass-paper. Remember that too heavy a use of glass-paper can rub out all those fine details which have so carefully been turned in. *(Fig.30.9).*

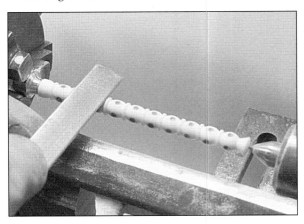

Fig. 30.9. Cleaning off the paint.

31 – Dyed Bone.

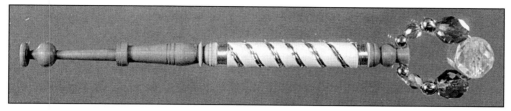

Fig. 31.1. Resist dyed bone.

Occasionally some pieces of bone are "fatty" which have discoloured areas where the fat has soaked in. This can look most unattractive but it is such a pity to waste a piece of bone so why not do that which the 19th century bobbin makers did — dye the bobbin.

I use Dylon permanent fabric dye. It needs to be quite strong. Use a Pyrex or enamel saucepan and mix in about a quarter of a litre (a half pint) of water to about a quarter of the small dye pot. The saucepan is then heated bringing the solution to a low boil. The bone bobbin is placed in the boiling dye for 30 secs. The dye solution may be kept for several "dippings" but as soon as it loses its strength then throw it out and mix fresh.

● Remember some of those broken pieces of bone bobbins? Well now we have a use for them. They may be used to test the strength of the dye. Throw a piece in then recover it to see whether more or less dye needs to be added to obtain the density of colour needed. This prevents wasting good turned bone bobbins.

● When satisfied that the dye is OK place the turned bobbins in the saucepan and leave them for about half a minute in the boiling dye. Lift them out — I use salad tongs — and place them on kitchen towel to dry.

● Before the bobbins are used it is advisable to thoroughly wash off the heads and necks in clean water rubbing them firmly with kitchen towel to ensure that there is no "loose" dye which may colour lace thread.

Here are two styles which look good when dyed.

Resist.

● The bobbin is turned — head and neck and body, but the central section is left thick and unturned. *(Template Fig.31.6).*

● This central section is then painted with french polish. This will prevent the dye from penetrating the bone protected beneath (blue dye is very difficult to keep out). *(Fig. 31.3).*

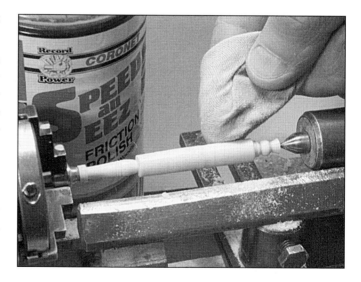

Fig. 31.3. Applying the resist.

● When the french polish resist is dry place the bobbin in the saucepan of boiling dye for half a minute then remove and allow it to dry.

● Replace the bobbin in the lathe turning away the unturned, resist painted, centre section. This should turn down to clear, clean bone. *(Fig. 31.4).*

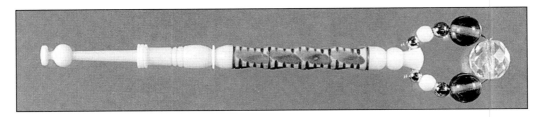

Fig. 31.2. Tutti Frutti.

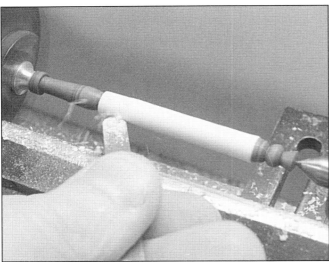

Fig. 31.4. Turning away the centre.

● If a wire groove is turned at either end and a spiral groove run up the middle section a most interesting effect may be achieved. *(Fig. 31.5).*

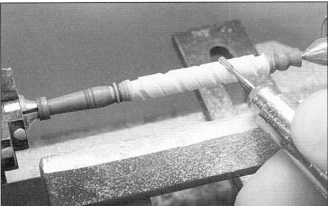

Fig. 31.5. Cutting the spirals.

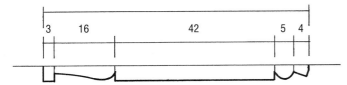

Fig. 31.6. Template resist.

Tutti-frutti. *(Fig 31.2).*

This is the reverse of the above.

● Turn the bobbin and decorate the centre section with a series of grooves *(Fig. 31.7)* cut using the corner of the square end tool. *(Template Fig.31.10).*

Fig. 31.7. Turning decorative grooves.

● Into the pendant drill fit a small rotary grinding stone. Hold it at an angle to the top surface of the bobbin body and across that centre section cutting four elliptical hollows into the grooved section. *(Fig. 31.8).*

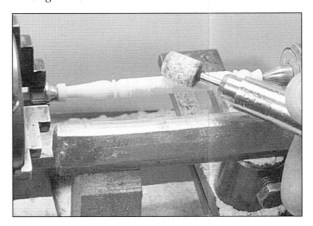

Fig. 31.8. Grinding the hollows.

- Repeat this process so that four sides of the bobbin are decorated in this way. A chuck jaw may be used as an index to help arrange the cuts evenly around the bobbin.

- Now instead of dipping the bobbin into the dye carefully paint the centre section with hot dye taking care to prevent the dye from running outside the decorated area. *(Fig. 31.9).*

- Set the bobbin on one side raising the bobbin horizontally between two blocks allowing it to dry. Any dye which runs over the decorated edge may be turned away but be prepared for that dye to have soaked deeply into the bone.

- A light sanding on the outer surface highlights the depth of colour in the ground away sections.

Fig. 31.9. Painting the dye.

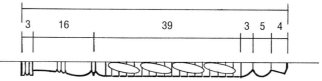

Fig. 31.10. Template for Tutti Frutti.

32 – Arrows.

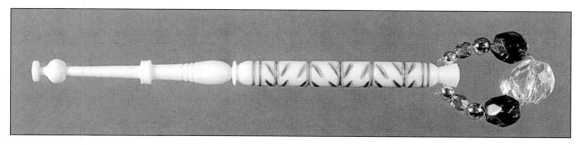

Fig. 32.1. Arrows.

A neat little bobbin with an interesting coloured decoration of rows of opposing arrows, but they must be carefully and precisely cut for it to look good.

- With the head and neck held in collets in the chuck turn the bobbin body as before.

- Using a pencil transfer the marks from the template to the rotating bobbin. *(Fig.32.2).*

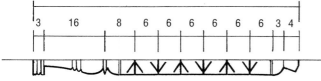

Fig. 32.2. Template.

- Cut the grooves, two at either end and one at each of the five marked positions, using the corner of the square end tool. *(Fig. 32.3).*

- Choose one chuck jaw to act as an index bringing it to 12 o'clock.

- Fit a flat fissure burr into the pendant drill.

- Starting at the first of the five grooves hold the burr at about 45 degrees, the top pointing to the left. Bring it down so that the lower edge touches the left side of the groove and make the cut.

- Repeat the cut on groove two but this time make the cut on the right hand side with the "top" of the burr making contact with the groove.

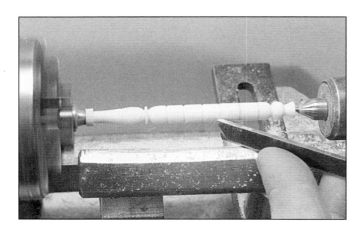

Fig. 32.3. Cutting the grooves.

- Move to groove three and make the angled burr cut on the left side as for groove one. *(Fig. 32.4).*

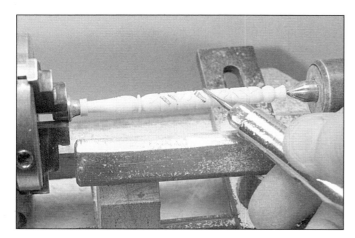

Fig. 32.4. Starting to cut the "arrows".

- Next work on the right hand side of groove four cutting with the burr in the same manner as for groove two.

- Finally cut on the left of groove five repeat the cut which was worked on groove one and three. *(Fig.32.5).*

- Turn the chuck so that the index jaw is at 3 o'clock and repeat the cuts.

- Work in a similar manner when the index jaw is moved to 6 o'clock and 9 o'clock.

- Return the index jaw to 12 o'clock and now turn the burr so that its tip points to the right and is set at 45 degrees to the work.

- Make the first cut to the right of groove one so that it makes a V shape against the cut already made on the opposite side.

- Move to groove two keeping the burr to the left of the groove. Make the next cut so that the tip touches the groove and mirrors the cut on the opposite side of the groove again making a V shape.

- Repeat the cut at groove three in the same manner as for groove one.

- The cut at groove four is a repeat of the one made at groove two.

- Finally make the cut on the right of groove five so that a V is made against the cut on the left of the groove — exactly the same as grooves one and three.

- Repeat these cuts with the index jaw at 3 o'clock, 6 o'clock and 9 o'clock.

It is necessary to make each of these burr cuts the same length and depth for this decoration to look good. Practice on some scrap bone to achieve the proficiency needed before moving on to an important piece.

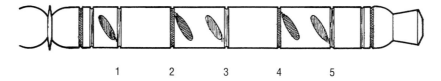

Fig. 32.5. Layout of the first cuts.

- All that remains is to paint in the grooves and burr cuts using Acrylic paint. *(Fig. 32.6).*

Fig. 32.6. Colouring in.

- Once the paint is dry it may be lightly filed clean to remove the majority of stray paint before being glass-papered smooth. *(Fig. 32.7).*

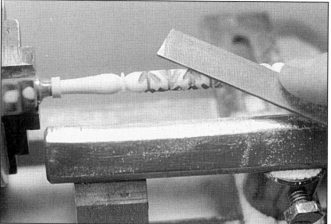

Fig. 32.7. Cleaning off.

33 – Tinsel & Wire.

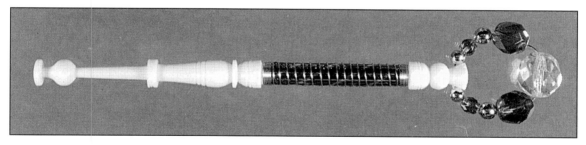

Fig. 33.1. Tinsel and wire.

The whole effect of this bobbin relies upon the choice of the tinsel held in the wide central band of the bobbin body. An open spiral of brass wire holds the tinsel in place protecting it from wear yet allowing it to be clearly seen. Early forms of this bobbin relied upon the brilliance of colour from the thin tin strips held captive by the wire. Unfortunately after over 100 years of use many of these early bobbins have lost their wire allowing the tinsel to be either worn away or to fall off.

- Hold the bobbin head and neck in a collet in the chuck jaws.
- Mark the important points on the rotating blank, in pencil, using the template as a guide. *(Fig.33.2).*

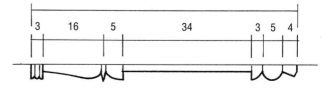

Fig. 33.2. Template.

- Turn the bobbin body as before.

- Mark out the extreme edges of the wide central band to be turned away.

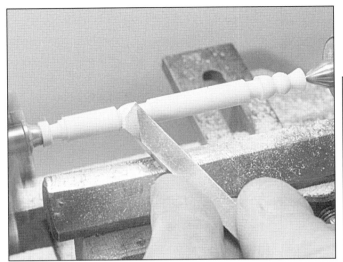

Fig. 33.3. Preparing the bobbin.

- Take the square end tool and turn a groove about 2mm ($^1/_{12}$ inch) deep on the inside of these marks.

- Next take a round nose tool and turn away the area between the two grooves maintaining that 2mm ($^1/_{12}$ inch) depth. *(Fig. 33.4).*

Fig. 33.4. Turning the central area.

- The base of this central area may be turned cleanly flat using the square end tool like a skew chisel. Hold it against the work at the extreme right hand end. Twist it slightly to the left and make a cut, moving to the left, to the far end of the central area. It may take a little practice but once mastered it is a useful technique. *(Fig. 33.5).*

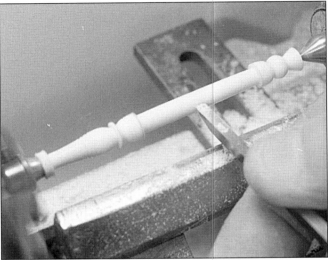

Fig. 33.5. Cleaning up the central area.

- Once this central area has been turned flat and true it can be decorated using tinsel and wire. The exact method is described in the chapter headed "Decorating Bobbins".

34 – Two Start Double Fairing.

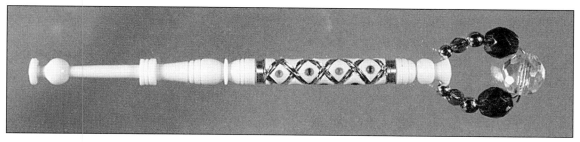

Fig. 34.1. Double start fairing.

Of all the forms of decoration this needs the greatest precision for any slight movement one way or the other when marking or cutting the grooves will cause the intersections to be off — set. This will be so noticeable that it will cause the bobbin to look most awkward and clumsy.

- Turn the bobbin as before with the head and neck supported in collets and held in the chuck. The template having been used to mark out important positions. *(Figs. 34.2 & 34.3).*

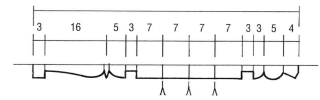

Fig. 34.2. Template.

- Using the square end tool turn the wire grooves in their marked positions either end of the bobbin's central section.

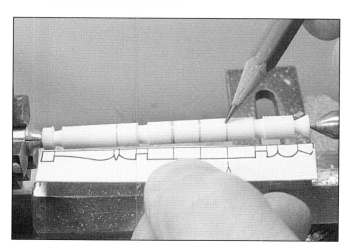

Fig. 34.3. Marking out the bobbin.

- This central section is to be divided with a pencil line, first in the centre, then those two sections divided in half. (Three lines dividing the centre section into four equal parts.) The lines numbered from the left to the right, 1,2 and 3.

- Choose a chuck jaw as a datum and bring it to 12 o'clock.

- Mark a pencil line from one wire groove to the other across the top of the bobbin. This is line A.

- Move the datum jaw to 6 o'clock and mark a second pencil line from one wire groove to the other across the now, new, top of the bobbin. This is line B.

> It is best to mark the spiral lines to be cut in pencil first, then follow that marked line with the junior hacksaw to produce the spiral cut. Once you have become proficient in cutting these lines then the spiral pencil marking can be done away with and only the pencil intersections need be used as a guide for the spiral cut.

- Begin marking in pencil where line A touches the edge of the right hand wire groove.

- Slowly rotate the chuck anti-clockwise by hand until the intersection of line B/3 comes around.

- These first two points should be joined.

- Continue from this point — still rotating the chuck anti-clockwise — until the intersection of line A/2 is joined.

Fig. 34.4. Cutting the right hand spiral.

● Move from this point — still rotating the chuck — until the intersection of line B/1 is joined.

● Finally, still rotating the chuck, move on to join the intersection of line A and the edge of the left hand wire groove.

● A right hand spiral will have been drawn around the bobbin.

● Repeat this process beginning at the point where line B. touches the edge of the right hand wire groove, still rotating the chuck anti-clockwise by hand.

● Join this point with line A/3, then to line B/2, then line A/1, and finally line B where it touches the edge of the left hand groove.

● Now two parallel right hand spirals will have been marked.

● It will be less confusing if each of these right hand spirals is followed with a cut using a junior hacksaw. So cut them now using the same technique as for a wired bobbin. *(Fig. 34.4).*

● Having cut the right hand spirals begin marking out, in pencil, the left hand spirals.

● Join the intersection of line A and the edge of the left hand groove to line B/1 — still rotating the chuck anti-clockwise.

● Next join to A/2, then join to B/3, finally move to the intersection of line A and the edge of the right hand wire groove.

● The first left hand spiral will have been marked. Interestingly it will be seen that the lines also cross on the sides as well as at the top.

● Now for the final left hand spiral line.

● Repeat the process but this time begin at the point where line B meets the edge of the left hand groove.

● Still rotating the chuck anti-clockwise join this point to line A/1 intersection, then to point B/2, next to point A/3, and finally the intersection of line B. and the edge of the right hand wire groove.

● Having marked the two left hand spirals they may now be carefully cut using a junior hacksaw. *(Fig. 34.5).*

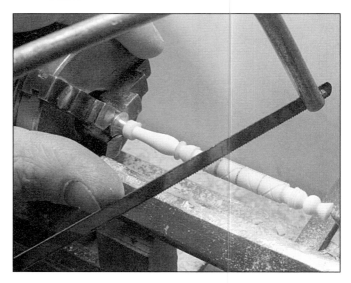

Fig. 34.5. Cutting the left hand spiral.

● It may be a little difficult for right handers, now you may have some sympathy for left handers a group of people who almost always have to conform.

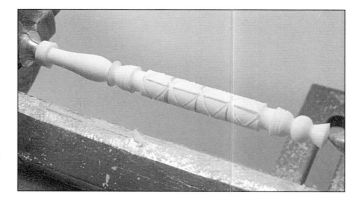

Fig. 34.6. The spirals cut.

- The spiral saw cuts may now be widened out using a flat fissure burr held in the pendant drill. This can be a little tricky so it might be advisable to practice on scrap pieces first.

- It is best to begin those spiral cuts considered the more difficult — the left hand spirals. *(Figs. 34.7 & 34.8).*

- Following the guide saw cuts, cut each spiral line with the burr keeping precisely on track.

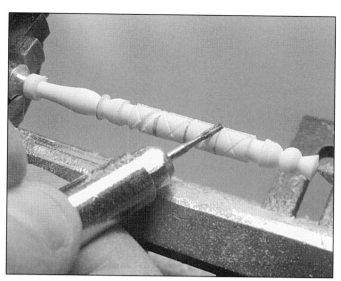

Fig. 34.8. Continuing the cut.

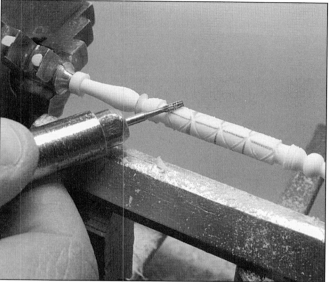

Fig. 34.7. Cutting the groove.

- Cut both left hand spiral grooves before moving to the right hand grooves.

- For the majority of workers who are right handed this will be the easiest way round. (Left handers reverse the process.) These right hand spirals will be a little bumpy for at each quarter turn another crossing will be met. This can be disconcerting and may throw the burr off track. This is the reason for cutting these grooves last for the right hand will have greater control.

- Carefully following the guide saw cuts on first, one right hand spiral track, then the other. *(Fig. 34.9).*

- Once all the grooves, both right and left spirals have been carefully cut, change the flat fissure burr for a round burr.

- At the exact centre of each diamond shaped island, between the grooves, drill a dot. *(Fig. 34.10).*

- When the paint has dried it can be cleaned off, and a final light sanding given to the whole bobbin.

- To learn how to add tinsel and decoration turn to the section — "Decorating Bobbins.

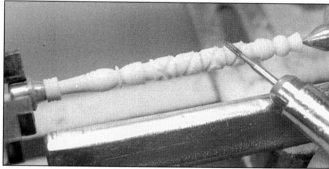

Fig. 34.9. The right hand groove.

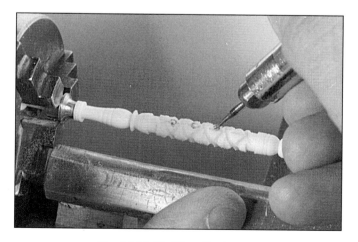

Fig. 34.10. Drilling the dots.

35 – Chevron Beaded.

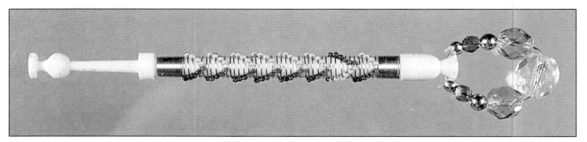

Fig. 35.1. Chevron beaded.

I t is important the beads used to decorate this bobbin are as small as possible. If the beads are heavy then the overall effect is destroyed.

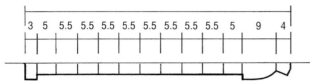

| 3 | 5 | 5.5 | 5.5 | 5.5 | 5.5 | 5.5 | 5.5 | 5.5 | 5.5 | 5 | 9 | 4 |

Fig. 35.2. Template.

● With the turned head and neck held in collets in the chuck transfer the marks from the template to the rotating plank using a pencil. (Figs.35.2 & 35.3).

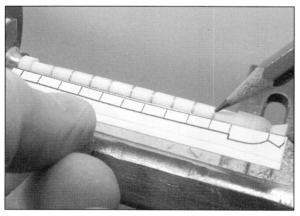

Fig. 35.3. Marking out.

● Turn the tail, round over down to the tail, then using the corner of the square end tool mark the two cut lines at the collar and the three close to the tail.

● Use the skew chisel to clean off the base of the tail.

● At the marked positions, top and bottom of the wire band to be turned away, cut a shallow groove (about 2mm [$^1/_{12}$ inch] deep) using the square end tool. Remember to move the tool very slightly from side to side to prevent the tool from gripping.

● Using the round nose tool turn away the area between the two grooves until it is flat and true. It may be finally cleaned up using the square end tool, at a slight angle, like a small skew as described earlier.

● This central section can now be marked out.

● Measure 4mm ($^1/_6$ inch) from the right hand end of the wide cut band and mark a pencil line — for reference call this line X.

● From the left hand end of the wide cut band measure in 4mm ($^1/_6$ inch) and mark a pencil line — line Y.

● The area between X and Y is now to be divided in half and a pencil line drawn around.

● Those two halves are divided and a pencil line drawn around.

● Those quarters are equally divided and a pencil line drawn around.

● This will produce seven lines and eight divisions between X & Y.

● Choose one chuck jaw to act as an index.

● Bring it to 12 o'clock and mark a pencil line from X to Y along the top.

● Move the index jaw to 3 o'clock and mark a second line on the top between X & Y.

● Rotate the bobbin so that a set of eight divisions can be seen.

● Take a pencil and draw a diagonal line through each box from top left to bottom right. (Fig.35.4).

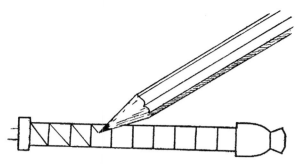

Fig. 35.4. *Marking the diagonals.*

- Rotate the chuck so that a second set of divisions can be seen.

- Move past this to the third set.

- Take a pencil and again draw a diagonal line through each box division from top left to bottom right.

- Rotate the chuck so that the fourth set of divisions are showing

- Take the pencil and draw diagonal lines in each box but this time from top right to bottom left.

- Turn the bobbin past the first marked set of divisions to the yet unmarked set and use a pencil to draw the diagonal lines in each box from top right to bottom left.

- When the four sections have been drawn in it will be seen that a series of V's or chevrons have been marked around the bobbin.

- Take a junior hacksaw (with the blade set backwards) and cut the marked pencil diagonals. Follow the same sequence that was used for marking out. This will ensure that the angles remain even. *(Fig. 35.5).*

Fig. 35.5. *Cutting the diagonals.*

- Make sure that the cuts meet top and bottom.

- The small cuts will be a little narrow. They can be widened slightly using the corner of a square needle file. (Fig. 35.6).

Fig. 35.6. *Filing the diagonals.*

- When all the diagonals have been cut and filed switch on the lathe and glass-paper away all the pencil marks.

- The precise details of beading this style of bobbin are given in the section "Decorating Bobbins", but remember when beading them if care and thought is given a wide variety of different effects may be achieved — eg. All the chevrons on one line the same colour, each chevron alternating in colour, multi — coloured chevrons, you could play for ever.

36 – Secret Bobbin.

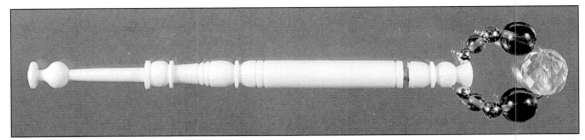

Fig. 36.1. Secret bobbin.

One of the fun things about lace bobbins are the tricks that can be played. What may look like a plain bobbin can hold a hidden secret. This simple bobbin has a secret compartment. One piece unscrews from the other. Screw threads can be satisfactorily cut on bone but they tend to be quite bulky. A simpler method of screwing together two sections is to use a metal thread fixing it in one part, the exposed thread can then be used to screw into the other section.

Visit your hardware store and select a small threaded bolt about 3mm ($^1/_8$ inch) diameter, and a tap which will match the thread of the small bolt. Also buy a tapping drill to match the thread size. I usually buy a 15mm ($^5/_8$ inch) long, 6BA brass bolt for I already have a tapping drill and matching tap.

● Take a piece of 100mm (4 inch) long piece of bone which has already been turned round.

● Cut, from one end, a 15mm ($^5/_8$ inch) piece.

● At the other end turn the head and neck.

● Measure from the top of the head down the body marking to a point 80mm (3 $^1/_8$ inch) away.

● Replace the longer piece in the chuck with the sawn end exposed, but with only a very short amount showing.

● Using a square end tool square off the end to the marked 80mm (3 $^1/_8$ inch) pencil line. Turn a small centre dimple in the end.

● Fix the tapping drill into the drill chuck and fit the drill chuck to the tailstock.

● Mark a point on the drill shank 30mm (1 $^3/_{16}$ inch) from the tip.

● Drill into the body to that marked depth. *(Fig. 36.2).*

● Withdraw the drill regularly to clear waste dust and to keep the work cool.

Fig. 36.2. Drilling out.

● Remove the drill from the chuck and replace it with the tap.

● Loosen the tailstock and bring it forward to the work held in the chuck.

● Rotate the chuck by hand and slowly push the tap into the drilled hole. It will be necessary to rotate the chuck $^1/_2$ a turn forwards followed by a $^1/_4$ turn back. This will allow the small pieces of bone cut away by the tap to fall free helping to cut a cleaner thread. *(Fig. 36.3).*

● Cut the thread inside to a full 9mm ($^3/_8$ inch) depth.

● When the thread has been cut inside, remove the piece from the chuck replacing it with the 15mm ($^5/_8$ inch) length. Again have the sawn end showing with only a small amount exposed.

● Square off the end and turn a small dimple into the face.

● Fit the tapping drill into the drill chuck and drill into this piece to a depth of 9mm ($^3/_8$ inch).

Fig. 36.3. Tapping the hole.

- Replace the drill with the tap and cut the thread in the end piece as before.

- Take the threaded bolt and saw off a 9mm ($^3/_8$ inch) length.

- Screw the sawn end into the 15mm ($^5/_8$ inch) end piece of bone to test the fit. Adjust where necessary by cleaning the metal thread or re-tapping the hole in the bone.

- When fully satisfied that a good fit has been achieved squeeze a small amount of supaglue into the tapped hole in the tail section. (Fig. 36.4).

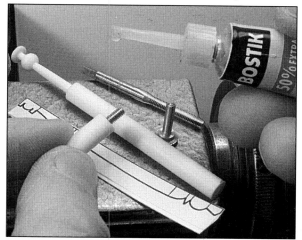

Fig. 36.4. Gluing the thread.

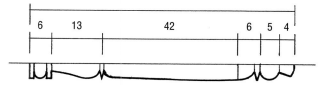

| 6 | 13 | 42 | 6 | 5 | 4 |

Fig. 36.5. Template.

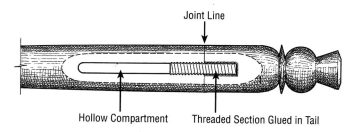

Fig. 36.6. Section through the bobbin.

- Screw in the metal thread until about 4mm ($^1/_6$ inch) is left exposed.

- Leave until the glue has fully dried.

- When absolutely sure that the glue has dried around the thread test the exposed metal thread in the tapped hole in the main body.

- When the fit is good, (adjust where necessary) the bobbin may be turned as any ordinary style of bobbin.

- Hold the head and neck in the collets in the chuck. Round the body using a square end tool, then transfer the marks from the template to the rotating blank and turn to shape. (Figs.36.5 & 36.7).

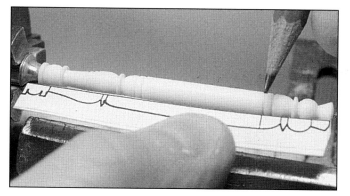

Fig. 36.7. Marking out.

- To disguise the joint use the corner of the square end tool to cut a groove over it.

- To disguise that groove cut several others along the body as decoration.

- To make the secret compartment more interesting make a tiny bobbin and hide it inside.

- Of course many forms of decoration can be used for this style of bobbin, but if wire is to be applied then make sure that any holes drilled through the body do not interfere with the screw thread or the hollow inside.

37 – Two Decker Mother & Babe.

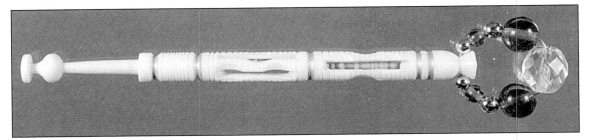

Fig. 37.1. Two decker mother and babe.

This two compartment mother and babe bobbin is a very popular style. It produces a very balanced design and shows off the bobbin maker's skill.

● In preparation turn a small piece of light coloured wood down to 3mm ($^1/_8$ inch) diameter, turning a 3mm ($^1/_8$ inch) length from its end. Set this "plug" safely on one side.

● Turn two baby bobbins each 9mm ($^3/_8$ inch) long and just under 3 mm ($^1/_8$ inch) diameter to fit inside the mother bobbin. (See the following section for details on turning miniature bobbins.)

● For this bobbin cut a 100mm (4 inch) length of bone and round to about 6mm ($^1/_4$ inch) diameter.

● Turn the head and neck on one end as usual.

● Turn the bobbin around in the chuck leaving about 40mm (1 $^1/_2$ inch) showing.

● Support the exposed end with a revolving centre held in the tailstock.

● Measure from the tailstock towards the headstock, first 9mm ($^3/_8$ inch), followed by 6mm ($^1/_4$ inch).

● Turn this 6mm ($^1/_4$ inch) section down to an accurate 3mm ($^1/_8$ inch) to match a drill of that size. *(Fig. 37.2).*

● This 15 mm ($^5/_8$ inch) length will be the plug to fit into the end of the bobbin.

● Saw off the 15mm ($^5/_8$ inch) section plug and set on one side.

● Loosen the chuck jaws and move the bobbin close to the chuck. Tighten the chuck jaws.

● Using a square end tool face off the end of the bone blank turning a tiny central dimple in its end. This will help start the drill on centre.

Fig. 37.2. Turning the plug.

● Remove the centre from the tailstock replacing it with a drill chuck holding a 3mm ($^1/_8$ inch) drill.

● Mark on the drill shank a position 45mm (1 $^3/_4$ inch) away from its cutting tip.

● Drill into the body of the bobbin to that marked depth. *(Fig. 37.3).*

Fig. 37.3. Drilling out.

> *When drilling into bone deeply it is essential to withdraw the drill regularly to clear out waste dust and to allow the tool to cool before returning to the drilling. If the drill bit becomes too hot the bone piece will become overheated and will crack.*

- When the depth is reached withdraw the drill replacing the drill chuck with the revolving centre.

- Test the plug in the drilled end of the bobbin.

- If it fits, fine, if it is too tight take a flat needle file and file around the plug until the fit is good.

- Remove the bobbin from the chuck. Take the collets and fit them around the head and neck and hold in the chuck.

- Support the tail end, with the plug now fitted, using the revolving centre in the tailstock.

- Now the body of the bobbin may be turned.

- Transfer the marks from the template to the revolving bobbin blank using a pencil. *(Figs. 37.4 & 37.5).*

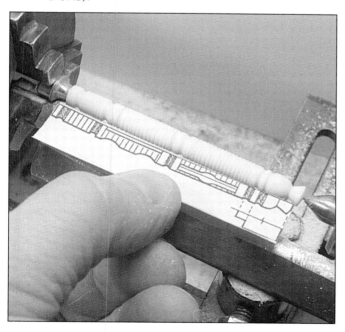

Fig. 37.4. Marking out.

- At the five marked areas — two close to the top, one between the window areas and two close to the tail — use a 3mm (1/8 inch) round nose tool to turn a shallow round bottomed groove. One of these grooves at the tail hides the plug joint line.

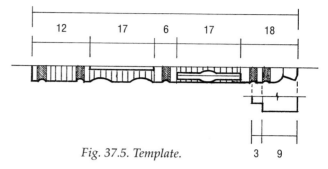

Fig. 37.5. Template.

- Between the top two grooves and across the window spaces cut a series of lines using the corner of the square end tool. These lines should be about 1mm ($^1/_{24}$ inch) apart.

- Before the windows are cut, mark in pencil, a datum line across the plug and body joint.

- Into the pendant drill fit a Dremel No. 199 saw cutter .(Or make one of your own, filing teeth into the edge of a small nail head.)

- The top set of windows closest to the head will be cut first.

- Choose one chuck jaw to act as an index.

- Begin with that jaw at 12 o'clock.

- With the saw cutter rotating bring it to the top of the first window section a little way away from the marked groove.

- Gently plunge the cutter into the work and draw it down towards the tail stopping a short distance from the middle shallow groove. In fact start at the top incised line and stop at the lower incised line.

- Lift the tool out and bring the index jaw to 3 o'clock.

- Carefully cut the second window in the same manner then lift the tool out. *(Fig. 37.6).*

- Set the index jaw to 6 o'clock. Cut the next window then move the jaw to 9 o'clock to cut the fourth window.

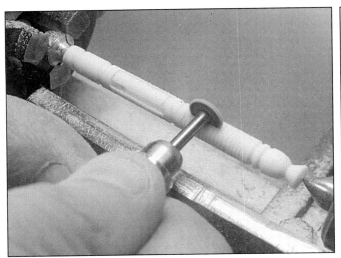

Fig. 37.6. Cutting the windows.

Fig. 37.7. Filing the windows.

> *When cutting the windows make sure that the cutter is cutting parallel to the body sides. Do not twist the cutter when cutting the window for this may shatter the bobbin. Always arrange that the cutter is cutting down (that the rotating teeth move down) into the work for an upward cut will often split the bone out. Always wear a mask to prevent the fine bone dust from being breathed in.*

- The lower four windows may now be cut in the marked section but this time cut them so that they are off-set from the windows above them. This will give the finished design a little "movement".

- Once all the windows have been cut take a flat needle file and clean out all the edges and tops and bottoms of all the windows.

- Starting with the top windows use a half round file to file a shallow groove top and bottom of window 1 and window 3. On windows 2 and 4 file a shallow groove across the middle.

- Now move to the bottom windows and again use the half round file to file a shallow groove top and bottom of windows 1 & 3. On windows 2 & 4 file a shallow groove across the middle. (*Fig. 37.7*).

- This small detail adds a great deal of interest.

- Withdraw the tailstock, remove the plug from the end of the bobbin.

- Slide the first babe, head first, inside the drilled hollow. (*Fig. 37.8*).

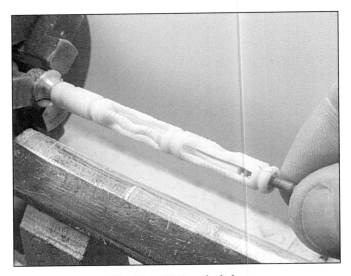

Fig. 37.8. Fitting the babe.

- Now find that tiny wooden plug which was turned earlier (3mm [^{1}/$_8$ inch] long, 3mm [^{1}/$_8$ inch] diameter) and push it up after the babe. (Use a round needle file or other small tool.) As the plug comes just to the top of the lower window, blocking it off from the other window, take a pin and run a tiny drop of supaglue on its tip. Now move the pin so that the glued tip touches the tiny wooden plug through one of the windows. The drop of supaglue will transfer from the pin to the plug. Immediately push the plug up into the area between the two windows, not so hard to cause it to show in the top window. This plug will keep the babe in the top window from dropping down into the lower one. (*Fig. 37.9*).

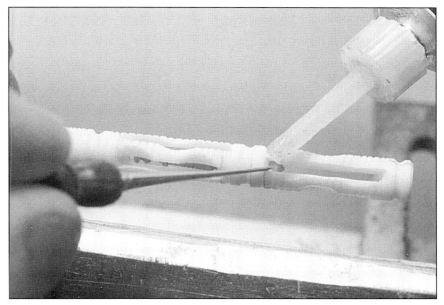

Fig. 37.9. Gluing the partition plug.

- Now take the second babe and fit it into the lower chamber.

- Mix a little epoxy resin glue, I use the rapid variety.

- Spread some mixed glue on the plug end (the 3mm [$^1/_8$ inch] diameter end) and push it into the body lining up the pencil datum marks. Do not let the glue squeeze up into the compartment for it may glue the babe in position.

- Bring the tailstock back and apply pressure whilst the glue dries. (Fig. 37.10).

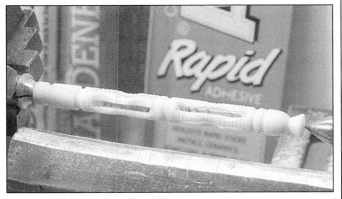

Fig. 37.10. Gluing the tail.

- When the glue has fully dried turn away the excess from the shallow groove around the joint.

- Lightly glass-paper the whole bobbin clean.

- Now to disguise the joint and also to add a sparkle to the bobbin take a little gold paint — designers gauche is excellent — and with the lathe running use a fine brush to colour in the five shallow grooves. (Fig. 37.11).

- Switch off the lathe, remove the bobbin and leave it to dry and then you will have a sparkling two decker mother and babe.

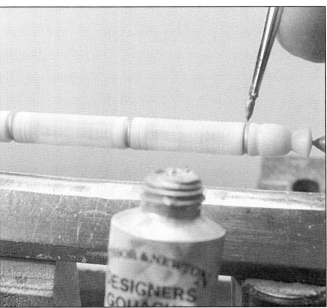

Fig. 37.11. Painting the bands.

38 – Turning Miniatures

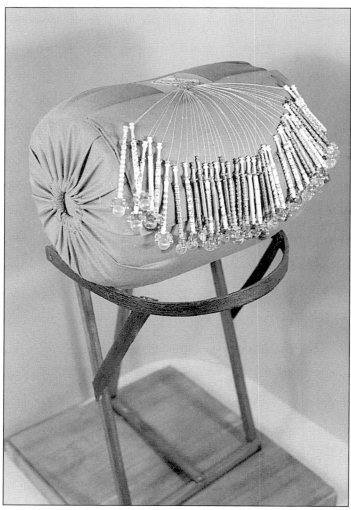

Fig. 38.1.
Miniature pillow and bobbins, 45cm. (18 inch) high.

● For intermediate size baby bobbins the piece is held in the chuck and the tail is supported with the revolving centre in the tailstock. *(Fig. 38.2).*

Fig. 38.2. Miniature square end tool and babe.

● For really tiny babes the piece is held in the chuck with a short, unsupported piece showing. This may be turned down to the required diameter at its end. The head can then be turned, a little more

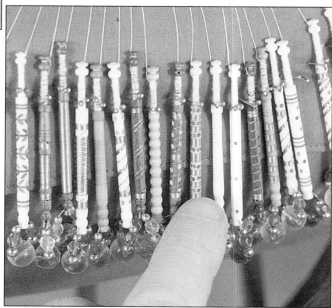

Fig. 38.3. Bobbins on miniature pillow.

Miniature bobbins may be turned to be used as babies in the mother & babe style of bobbin, for earrings, necklaces or even for a scale version of a lace pillow. *(Fig. 38.1).*

The techniques used for turning miniatures are no different from those used when turning full size lace bobbins, but I do encourage the use of smaller tools for it is far easier to reach into finer recesses with finer tools. Miniatures may be satisfactorily turned with large tools but it is doing the job the awkward way.

is then rounded down to diameter to allow the neck to be turned followed by a little more for the body. The complete tiny bobbin can then be parted off. (The bobbin can of course be turned tail first if wished.) There is no limit to the fineness of turning that may be achieved, just take the work slowly and carefully. *(Figs. 38.4 & 38.7).*

● When dealing with turning in miniature it is important to maintain the proportion of the bobbin. Don't just turn the bobbin shorter, remember to reduce its diameter precisely to match its reduced length. Remember also to scale the head and neck to the body size. I have seen so many small bobbins which have attempted to be miniatures but have failed miserably because they were too dumpy or completely out of proportion.

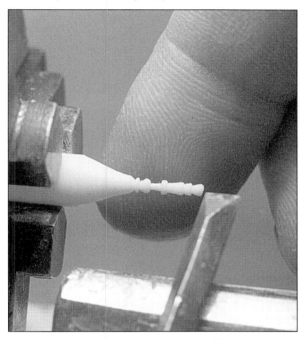

Fig. 38.4. Miniature skew and babe.

● These miniature bobbins need not be wholly plain. There is no reason why they should not be decorated in a similar manner to the full sized versions. Do be careful, if decorating with wire or beads, to ensure that the thickness of the wire and the diameter of the beads are to scale for thick wire and large beads will ruin the effect. *(Figs. 38.3 & 38.5).*

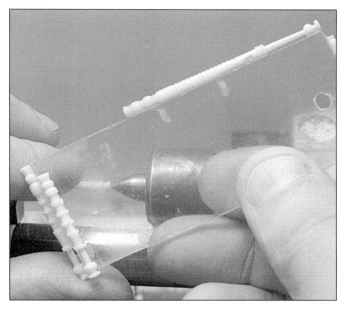

Fig. 38.6. Template — babes glued to perspex.

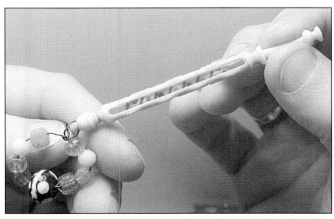

Fig. 38.5. Decorative babe inside bobbin.

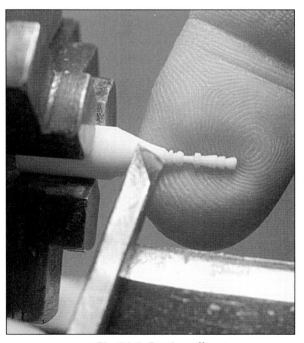

Fig. 38.7. Parting off.

Scaling.

It is so simple to scale a bobbin down.

1. Take a piece of card and mark, from its left hand corner, the chosen length of the miniature bobbin.

2. Take the full size bobbin which is to be reduced in size and lay it on the workbench with its head to the right and its tail to the left. A piece of Blu-tak will hold it in place preventing it from rolling off the bench. *(Fig. 38.8).*

3. Stand about 1 metre (3 feet) away from the workbench. Close one eye holding the card between the bobbin and open eye.

4. Line up the left hand corner of the card with the tail of the bobbin and move the card either towards the bobbin or closer to the eye until the right hand mark on the card lines up with the top of the head. The left hand end of the card should still be lined up with the tail.

5. Use a pencil to mark the important points on the card matching those positions on the bobbin. The photograph shows a very scratchy drawing on the card but this is often the way it will be first drawn, it can now the tidied up. *(Fig. 38.9).*

6. Lay the card on the workbench and lightly draw in the bobbin shape according to the marks. This will ensure that there will be no confusion concerning the marked points.

● The card template may then be used to mark out the miniature bobbin and the bobbin can then the turned. I usually use a turned baby bobbin and glue it to a small piece of perspex and use that as the template. *(Fig. 38.6).*

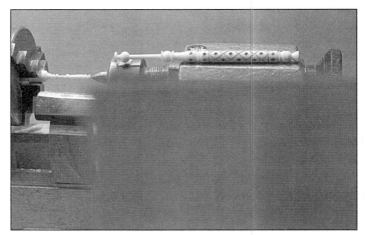

Fig. 38.8. Scaling.

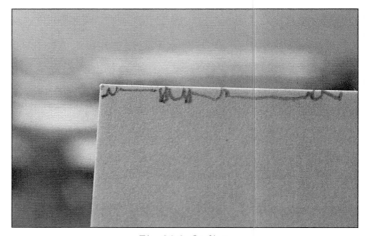

Fig. 38.9. Scaling.

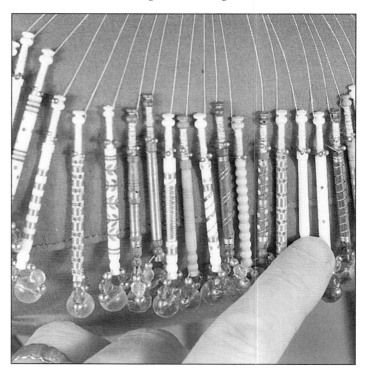

Fig. 38.10. More miniatures from the pillow.

39 – Grandmother Bobbin.

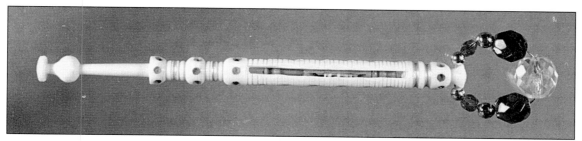

Fig. 39.1. Grandmother.

The Grandmother bobbin requires careful work and a delicate touch. It is no more than 6mm ($^1/_4$ inch) diameter when finished yet contains a baby bobbin which has a baby inside it.

I always begin these bobbins by turning the grandbabe then move on to the babe finally producing the grandmother. This will allow the whole bobbin to be assembled while the grandmother is held in the lathe. The grandmother bobbin then remains running true and on centre allowing the final, decorative, gold paint bands to be applied cleanly and accurately.

When turning the grandbabe and the mother bobbins use the very small skew and square end tools.

The templates for all three parts can be seen in *Fig.39.2.*

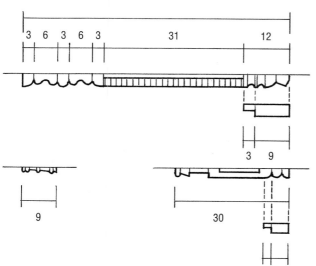

Fig. 39.2. Template.

Turning The Grandbabe.

● This babe is about 8mm ($^3/_8$ inch) long and 1.5mm ($^1/_{16}$ inch) diameter so choose a piece of bone a little longer and a little thicker from which to turn this piece.

● Set the piece of bone in the chuck so that about 12 mm ($^1/_2$ inch) is showing.

● Using the round nose tool turn the first 3mm ($^1/_8$ inch) down to the set diameter. *(Fig. 39.3).*

Fig. 39.3. Marking out the babe.

● On its end carefully turn the head and part of the neck using a fine skew chisel. *(Fig. 39.4).*

Fig. 39.4. Miniature skew.

- Again using the round nose tool carefully turn down another 3mm ($^1/_8$ inch) length to 1.5mm ($^1/_{16}$ inch) diameter and continue turning the neck, the collar, then part of the body. *(Fig. 39.5).*

Fig. 39.5. Turning the body.

- The remaining part of the babe may be turned down to diameter.

- The tail may then be shaped.

- Once satisfied with the shape the tiny bobbin may be parted off using the skew chisel. *(Fig. 39.6).*

- When parting off lightly support the right hand end in the fingers this will prevent the tiny bobbin flying off into the bone dust and becoming lost.

Fig. 39.6. Parting off.

- The grandbabe must be placed somewhere safe, and that means a safe place where it will be found again. Too often have I placed my tiny turned bobbin down "safely" and had to search madly when I needed it some time later.

One of the many benefits of turning grandmother bobbins is that many of the smaller "unusable" pieces of bone now have a use so select from that box full a piece about 50mm (2 inch) long and set it in the chuck supporting the right hand end with a revolving centre.

The Mother Bobbin.

Although this bobbin is on a much smaller scale than other mother bobbins the techniques used to produce it are exactly be same as those used previously.

- Using the round nose tool turn the whole piece lightly down to about 5mm ($^1/_5$ inch) diameter.

- Using the card template mark the tail plug on its end turning the stopper section out to 2mm ($^1/_{12}$ inch) diameter. Mark a pencil datum line across the plug and the body.

- Loosen the chuck jaws and draw the body back into the chuck until the plug and a little piece more is showing. Tighten the chuck jaws. Saw the plug from the main part of the blank and set it aside safely.

● Face off the end of the blank.

● In the drill chuck fit a 2mm ($^1/_{12}$ inch) drill. Mark on its shank a position 14mm ($^7/_{12}$ inch) from its cutting point. Fit the drill chuck to the tailstock.

● Carefully drill into the blank to the marked depth.

● Withdraw the drill. Remove the chuck from the tailstock and replace it with the revolving centre. *(Fig. 39.7).*

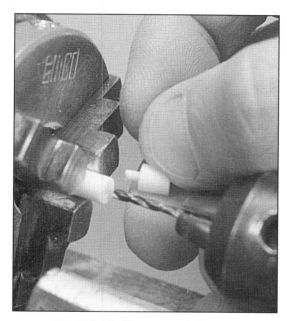

Fig. 39.7. Drilling out and the plug.

● Fit the plug into the drill hole aligning the datum lines. If the plug is tight use a flat needle file and lightly file the end until a good fit is achieved.

● Loosen the chuck jaws and bring the blank forward to its original position. Support the plug end with the revolving centre.

● Now very carefully turn the blank down to 4mm ($^1/_6$ inch) diameter.

Use the round nose tool to make very light and clean cuts when turning these small pieces. Too heavy a cut may cause the piece to twist and shatter around the drilled out hollow centre section.

● Using the card template mark out the important points then begin turning the tail. Use the corner of the square end tool to cut a shallow groove at the joint between the tail and the body. This will disguise the joint.

● Mark, in pencil, the start and finish points of the window openings in the body of the bobbin.

● Turn the neck with care then complete the head.

If you are able, then buy the small arbor and fine slitting saw as shown in the photograph. In fact I fit about three fine saw blades together in the arbor and cut the window opening in one pass. If you cannot find the fine saw blades then I know that small circular grinding discs similar to saw blades are available, they will fit in the arbor and cut satisfactory windows.

● Use the saw blades to cut the four windows. Each window is cut into the body of the bobbin starting at one marked pencil line at the neck end and finishing at the marked pencil line at the tail end. Again one chuck jaw is used as an index and the four points on the clock are used to set the positions for the windows. *(Fig. 39.8).*

Fig. 39.8. Cutting the windows.

- When the windows have been cut and the bobbin has been lightly glass-papered it may be parted off using the skew. Gently support the bobbin in the fingers of the right hand whilst carefully slicing to the left of the bobbin head.

- When the bobbin is cut free there is no safer place to leave it than in a small bath of red dye. (Fig. 39.9).

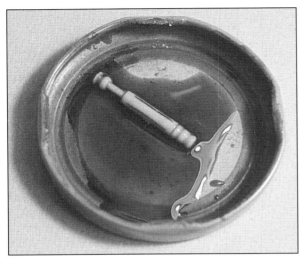

Fig. 39.9. Dying the babe.

- Dying this mother bobbin red makes it more easily seen inside the grandmother and also makes the tiny white grandbabe, which fits inside it, more visible. Use the lid from the jar of dye as a small bath. I leave the bobbin soaking for the time it takes me to make the grandmother.

The Grandmother.

- Take a 100mm (4 inch) length of thick rounded bone.

- Turn the head and neck.

- Reverse the piece in the lathe leaving about 30mm (1 $^1/_8$ inch) showing. The end is supported using the revolving centre.

- Mark out the plug, the stopper section being about 5mm ($^1/_5$ inch) long.

- Turn this stopper section down to 4.2mm ($^1/_6$ inch) diameter.

- Mark a pencil datum line across the plug and body then cut the whole plug away from the main body. Set it aside safely, maybe with the grandbabe.

- Face off the end of the blank using a square end tool.

- Into the drill chuck fit a 4.2mm ($^1/_6$ inch) drill bit and mark a position 40mm (1 $^9/_{16}$ inch) along its shank from the cutting point.

- Drill into the body of the bobbin to this marked depth. (Fig. 39.10).

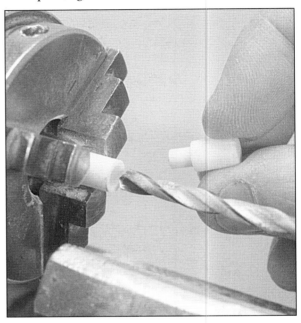

Fig. 39.10. Drilling out and the plug.

Remember to withdraw the drill regularly to remove bone dust and to allow the drill to cool slightly. If the bone bobbin is overheated when being drilled it will crack.

- Withdraw the drill, set it and the chuck to one side replacing the revolving centre in the tailstock.

- Bring the plug to the bobbin blank and fit it in place. Use a needle file to clean the stopper to size if need be.

- Loosen the chuck jaws and remove the bobbin repositioning it so that the head and neck are held in collets in the chuck. Support the tail with the revolving centre.

- Lightly and carefully, using a round nose tool, turn the bobbin body down to 6mm ($^1/_4$ inch) diameter or under.

- With the work rotating use a pencil to transfer the marks from the template to the bobbin.

- Turn the tail first using a square end tool then take the skew chisel to face off the tail end.

- Round the end of the bobbin down to the tail.

- The two hollow grooves, one to conceal the plug/body joint the other as decoration, may be shaped using the skew or a small, 3mm (^{1}/$_8$ inch), round nose tool.

- Between the two pencil boundary marks of the window area use the corner of the square end tool to cut a series of lines about 1mm (^{1}/$_{24}$ inch) apart. Not too deep for there is a hollow beneath.

- Using a small grinding burr held in the pendant drill, grind a series of hollows on each of the four sides of the bobbin in a manner similar to that shown in dyed bobbins Ch. 31. *(Fig. 39.11).*

Fig. 39.11. Grinding burr in use.

- At the head end the skew may be used to shape the bulb in the centre and the rounded ends at either side. The beads and cove between them may be shaped. Some may find it easier to remove the majority of material here using a small, 3mm (^{1}/$_8$ inch), round nose tool.

- Once all the turning as been completed fit a round burr into the pendant drill.

> *Drilled dots will be cut on the bulb of the tail and the three bulb areas at the head. To ensure that these dots all fall in line, with the lathe running, mark a centre line in pencil around those points. The drilled dots can then be spaced neatly along that marked line.*

- These drilled dots will be set against each of the three jaws, (the jaws acting as index points) then dots set between those points. So bring one jaw to 12 o'clock and drill dot the top position on the three bulbs at the front and the tail bulb on the marked line. Bring the second jaw to 12 o'clock and repeat. Bring the first jaw to 12 o'clock and drill dot again.

- At the points between those three drill dotted areas use the burr to create hollow dots.

- The windows will be cut using the same tool which was used to cut other mother and babe windows. (Dremel tool No. 199 or a specially shaped nail head.)

- Take one jaw as an index and bring it to 12 o'clock.

- With the tool rotating, gently plunge it into the top of the bobbin just to the right of the left hand pencil mark which marks the start of the window.

- Move the rotating tool, carefully to the right out towards the pencil mark close to the tail which is the end of the window. *(Fig. 39.12).*

> *Those lines cut in by the corner of the square end tool not only decorate the bobbin body but they also help prevent the bone from chipping out at the start and end of the cut.*

- When the first window has been cut move the index jaw to 3 o'clock repeating the process.

- Again cut windows when the index jaw is at 6 o'clock and then at 9 o'clock.

- Lightly glass-paper the bobbin then mark a slight pencil datum line across the plug and body.

- Whilst the drill dots are being coloured in the mother bobbin may be removed from the dye, laid on kitchen towel and allowed to dry.

- The red dyed mother must be fully dry inside and out before the tiny grandbabe is slid in.

- The tail end may be glued in place using supaglue. Take great care to re-align the tail precisely.

- Take the now filled, red dyed, mother bobbin to the grandmother held in the lathe.

- Withdraw the tailstock and remove the plug then slide the mother bobbin inside.

- Using rapid setting epoxy adhesive glue the plug back in position bringing the datum lines together.

- Bring the centre up to apply pressure on the tail whilst the glue sets.

- Returning later once the glue is dry turn away the dry squeezed out glue then glass-paper the

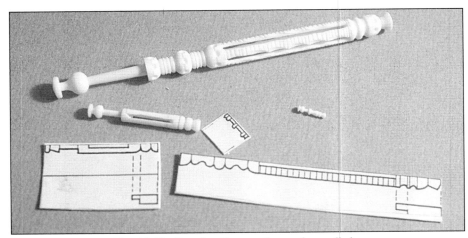

Fig. 39.13. Grandmother, mother and grandbabe.

whole bobbin clean. Make sure that the areas around the painted dots are cleaned of any stray paint marks.

- The four coves, one turned to disguise the plug joint and the other three for decoration, may now be coloured in.

- With the lathe running apply gold paint to the four coves. I use designers gauche which gives a good deep gold colour and is easily applied.

- Switch off the lathe and leave the paint to dry.

- Once dry the tail may be drilled and the grandmother bobbin spangled.

> *The windows I have left plain but they may be decorated with a deeper ribbed pattern using a half round file which is used to cut across at an angle before the windows have been cut through. This will make the centre area a little weaker when cutting the windows so it is best to begin with plain windows and work up to the more decorative type.*

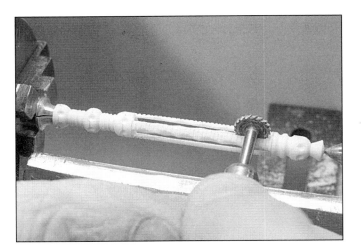

Fig. 39.12. Cutting the windows.

Fig. 39.14. A superb antique bone mother and babe bobbin with loose rings.

Part 4
Other Styles

Various continental style bobbins.

40 – Continental style

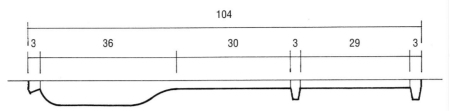

Fig. 40.1. Template.

The lace bobbins used on the European continent were, on the whole, plain functional tools in comparison with those used in England. Here I will describe the method of turning a general "continental" bobbin. There are many varied regional differences in these bobbins and they may be discovered by looking at any of the lacemaking books now available. The method of turning these will be much the same as described here.

As these bobbins are plain it is the ideal opportunity to use a more showy wood.

Turning the bobbin.

Unlike the East Midland bobbins I turn these in one go.

- Cut a 130mm (5 $^1/_8$ inch) length of wood, 18mm ($^3/_4$ inch) square. Turn the whole piece down to about 15mm ($^5/_8$ inch) diameter . Mark the head and neck at the tailstock end. *(Template Fig.40.1).*

- Using the square end tool turn into the workpiece at the start and finish of the neck down to 4mm ($^1/_6$ inch) diameter. Always widen the cut made by the square end tool to prevent it gripping.

- Use the gouge to remove the majority of the waste between those two points.

- Complete the neck using the square end tool as a small skew. Tilt the tool slightly to the right then slice along the neck to the right. Complete the neck so that it is clean and smooth.

- Take the square end tool and cut a groove to the left of the neck leaving a small collar, about 2mm ($^1/_{12}$ inch) wide, standing proud. Again turn down to 4mm ($^1/_6$ inch) diameter.

- The base of this groove should be cleanly cut in the same manner that the grooves were cut which marked the start and finish of the neck.

- Take the gouge and make a cut which sweeps down from the "bulb" of the bobbin into this marked groove.

- Continue cutting with the gouge until the required shape is achieved.

- This shape may be refined using the skew chisel.

- The small tail may now be turned to its angled shape using the square end tool first to cut a groove, again down to 4mm ($^1/_6$ inch) diameter, then cut at a slight angle to produce the tail shaping.

- Use the skew chisel to turn over the end of the bulb down to meet the tail.

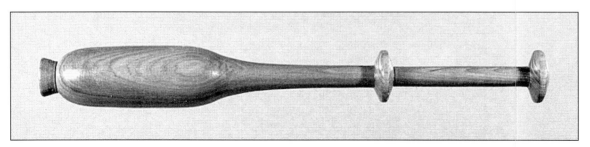

Fig. 40.2. Continental bobbin.

- With the skew still in hand turn the angled edges on either side of the collars at the top and the bottom of the neck.

- Lightly glass-paper the bobbin, do not rub out the sharp edges, then polish to a hard gloss.

- Part off at the left hand end of the tail. *(Fig. 40.3).*

- Touch a little polish on the parted off end of the bobbin to complete.

Fig. 40.3. Parting off the continental.

41 – Devon (Or Honiton) Bobbin.
Made in snakewood.

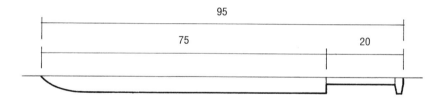

Fig. 41.1. Template.

Devon or Honiton bobbins, as they are better known, are used for making Honiton lace. Whilst this form of lace is being made the bobbins are passed through, round and under the threads being worked so it is necessary that they are smooth and that they have a pointed end to make this process easier.

The basic Honiton bobbin is made in one so collets are not used.

- Take a 110mm (4 $^1/_2$ inch) long, 6mm ($^1/_4$ inch) round piece of wood and hold it in the chuck supporting the end using a revolving centre.

- Lightly skim the blank, using a gouge, so that it is smooth and running on centre.

- Mark out in pencil the major points from the template whilst the blank is rotating. *(Fig.41.2).*

- Use a square end tool to turn down to 3mm ($^1/_8$ inch) diameter at the marked shoulder and also

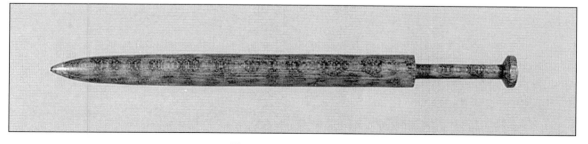

Fig. 41.2. Honiton bobbin.

beneath the rim-like head close to the tailstock. Complete the shaping on the neck using the square end tool like a small skew.

● To give the bobbin a more pleasing shape slightly taper the neck of the bobbin from the body down to the head at the tailstock end.

● Take the skew chisel and carefully make a light angled cut on the top of the head down to the revolving centre.

● Move to the other end of the head making another angled cut down to the neck.

● Before moving on lightly touch a piece of worn glass-paper to the head to rub out any sharp edges which may cut lace thread.

● Again using the skew work from two thirds down the body towards the marked end of the bobbin at the headstock end. Gently slice down to this mark creating a fluent curve towards a pointed end.

● Do not cut too deeply at this pointed end before lightly glass-papering and polishing.

Fig. 41.3. Parting off.

● Once the bobbin has been polished continue the shaping of the point removing as little of the polished area as possible. Part off the bobbin to a neat point. *(Fig. 41.3)*.

● Touch the unpolished point with a spot of polish to finish.

If you do decide to make Honiton bobbins then you would be well advised to talk to some Honiton lacemakers to help you decide upon the best shape to turn. Some like pointed ends, some like them blunt, some like the bobbin fat whilst others like them slim.

Branscombe Riggled.

Made in Boxwood. *(Fig. 41.5)*.

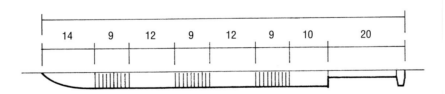

Fig. 41.4. Template for Branscombe riggled.

In Branscombe, Devon, many of the bobbins were decorated with a series of wax filled grooves, they were given the name of riggled bobbins (a corruption of ridged).

For this style it is necessary to use a dense hardwood such as Boxwood. The dense wood will not allow the coloured wax from soaking into the surrounding wood.

● Produce the basic shape as described earlier but do not part off.

● Transfer the groove marks from the template to the rotating Honiton bobbin using a pencil. *(Fig.41.4)*.

● Use the corner of a square end tool to mark the series of grooves. *(Fig. 41.7)*.

● Polish the bobbin.

● Take a piece of sealing wax, place it in a clean jam jar, pour enough methylated spirits into the jar to part cover the wax. Leave until the wax has dissolved into a thick paste.

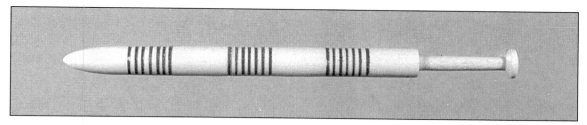

Fig. 41.5. Branscombe riggled.

- Using the end of a small screwdriver apply the wax paste to the groove area filling in the grooves completely. Try to avoid spreading the wax over other parts of the bobbin body. *(Fig. 41.6)*.

- Leave the wax to dry overnight.

- Only once the wax is fully dry should you try to remove the excess.

- Very carefully, using a skew chisel, turn away dry sealing wax but do not turn any of the wood away. *(Fig. 41.8)*.

> *If any of the sealing wax is torn out of the grooves it can be replaced with fresh soft wax but it must be left to harden before it is re-worked.*

- Remove the final small pieces of wax using glass-paper, then polish carefully.

- Part off using the skew chisel remembering to keep the pointed end of the bobbin nicely shaped.

- Finally polish that small tip of the bobbin to complete.

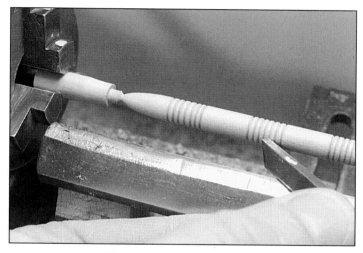

Fig. 41.7. Cutting the grooves.

Fig. 41.8. Cleaning off the bobbin.

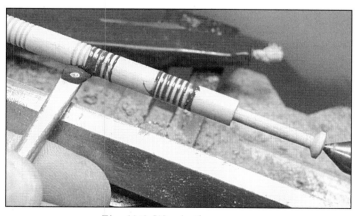

Fig. 41.6. Wax in the grooves.

Part 5
Decorating Bobbins

Fig. 42.1. Long nose pliers, end nips, Bostik, tinsel, foil, fine beads and wire.

42 – Decorating Bobbins.

The following tools and materials are required.

- One pair of long nose pliers.

- One pair of end nip pliers or nail clippers.

- A tube of quick drying glue such as Bostik clear.

- Tinsel (coloured plastic foil wrapping paper).

- Paper backed gold foil wrapping paper.

- A selection of extremely fine beads.

- Brass wire —26 gauge soft temper bright drawn — for general use.

  — 30 gauge soft temper bright drawn — for use with fine beads.

> *Brass wire is best for decorating bobbins as it resists tarnishing. Copper wire is acceptable but it dulls quickly. Avoid steel wire for it is difficult to use and will rust. Silver wire works well and looks attractive. Wire can be "straightened" by pulling it through a wad of cloth. Do not use wire which has a kink in it for it is at these weak points that wire will break.*

1. Wire Wrapping A Bobbin.

Here I will describe how to wire wrap a candy wired bobbin. It will also cover the wire wrapping of other styles of bobbin.

- First drill a 1mm ($1/24$ inch) hole at the start and finish of only one of the parallel saw cuts.

- This will be the start and finish of the first stage of wrapping.

- Next drill a 1mm ($1/24$ inch) hole at the tail end of the lower wire groove and the head end of the upper wire groove.

- Sit close to a table with all the material and equipment close to hand.

- Take a length of 26 gauge wire.

- If the wire is attached to the reel the reel may be trapped using the feet which can be used to hold

the wire in tension and also allow the wire to be unwound slowly when needed.

- If the wire is a cut length then either arrange for someone to hold the end or fix the end to some immovable object.

- At the closest end bend a small 4mm ($1/6$ inch) right angled "hook" using the pliers *(Fig 42.2)*.

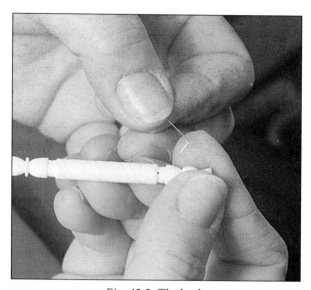

Fig. 42.2. The hook.

First I will deal with the parallel saw cut that has holes drilled at the start and finish .

- Take the "hook" of wire and push it into the drilled hole at the lower end of the parallel saw cut.

- Hold the bobbin so that the wire is in line with the saw cut and then pull gently, tensioning the wire.

- Twist the bobbin anti-clockwise and the wire will run into the saw cut. *(Fig. 42.3)*.

- When the full length of the saw cut has been filled stop but maintain the tension on the wire.

- Place a left index finger over the wire where the saw cut reaches the top of the wire groove. This will maintain wire tension whilst the end nips are used to cut the wire 50mm (2 inch) away from that position.

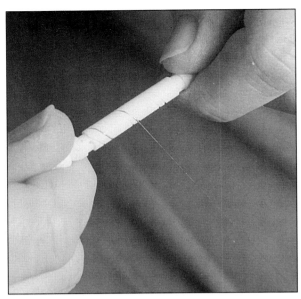

Fig. 42.3. Winding the wire.

● Take the pliers and grip the cut end of the wire. Maintain tension and bring the wire end to the drilled hole at the top of the saw cut. Thread the cut end of the wire down through the hole (the left index finger is still on the wire) and as it appears on the other side grip it and carefully pull it through tensioning firmly. Do not allow the wire to kink. *(Fig. 42.4).*

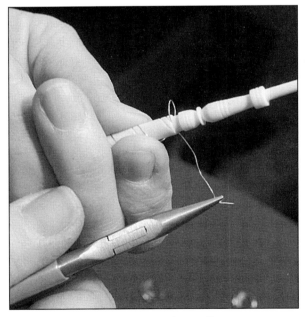

Fig. 42.4. Finishing off.

● The left index finger may now be released and the wire which protrudes from the underside may be clipped off flush.

● To complete the wiring of this bobbin again bend a small hook in the end of the wire.

● Thread it through the drilled hole at the tail end of the lower wire groove.

● Pull the bobbin and that will tension the wire.

● Twist the bobbin anti-clockwise and wrap the wire around filling that lower wire groove. Make sure that the wire packs against itself filling the wire groove completely. Keep turning the bobbin until the start of the unfilled parallel wire groove is reached, then angle the bobbin so that the wire falls in line with the saw cut.

● Twist the bobbin and wind the wire up in the saw cut until the top wire groove is reached.

● Continue wrapping around and fill the top wire groove.

● When the top wire groove is neatly filled manoeuvre the wire so that the last drilled hole can be seen — maintain tension — place the left index finger on the wire. Clip off the wire 50mm (2 inch) away.

● Take the pliers and grip the cut end of the wire then thread it down through the drilled hole.

● When the wire shows through the opposite side grip the end with the pliers and pull firmly — do not allow the wire to kink and remember to keep the wire well tensioned around the wire groove.

● Clip off the excess wire close to the bobbin.

● The bobbin now has its wire wrapping.

As all other forms of wire decoration follow this method of starting, maintaining tension, threading through, and finishing off, details will not be repeated when describing other forms of decoration which are based upon wiring.

2. Fairing.

● Measure the width of the groove which has been cut up the bobbin body. The groove which I cut is 1.5mm ($^1/_{16}$ inch).

● Cut a ribbon of tinsel, whose width matches that of the groove cut, about 30cm (1 foot) long. You may wish to begin with a shorter length until you become proficient.

● Touch a little glue in the cut groove where it meets the lower wire groove.

● Press the start of the tinsel onto the glue and line it up with the groove.

● Take the wire, bend the end and fix it into the drilled hold at the base of the tail end wire groove. *(Fig. 42.5).*

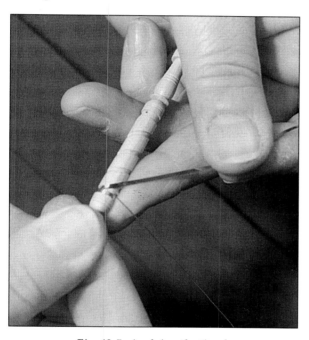

Fig. 42.5. Applying the tinsel.

● Turn the bobbin anti-clockwise wrapping the wire into the groove. When the wire groove is full move to the start of the spiral groove. The tinsel may well have wrapped itself awkwardly around the bobbin. Maintaining tension on the wire carefully unwrap the tinsel and line it up with the groove.

● Twist the bobbin so that the wire lines up with the groove and begin wrapping wire up that groove trapping the tinsel. *(Fig. 42.6).*

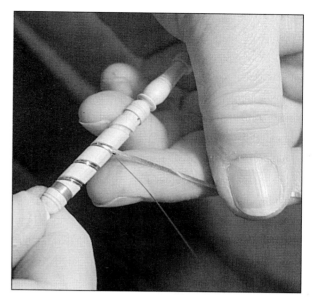

Fig. 42.6. Wrapping the tinsel.

● When the top of the groove is reached cut off the excess tinsel then wrap the wire into the groove finishing off as described earlier. *(Fig. 42.7).*

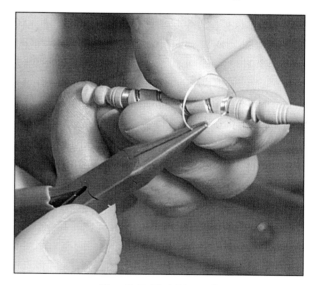

Fig. 42.7. Finishing off.

3. Double Fairing.

The double fairing decoration is a mixture of techniques from the candy wired bobbin and the fairing bobbin.

● Small holes for wire are drilled at the top and bottom of the left hand spiral groove.

● Holes are also drilled at the bottom end of the lower wire groove and at the top of the upper wire groove.

- The left hand spiral groove is the first to be decorated with tinsel and wire.

- The tinsel is lightly glued in place at the start of the lower end of the left hand spiral groove. The wire is bent at the end and pushed through the tinsel into the drilled hole beneath.

- The tinsel is wound up the left hand spiral groove and overlaid with wire.

- When the top of this groove is reached the wire is cut 50mm (2 inch) away from the groove end. The cut wire end is then pushed through the tinsel and threaded through the drilled hole. The wire is gripped with a pair of pliers as it shows through the bobbin on the opposite side. The wire is then pulled tight and the excess is clipped off.

- All that remains is to wrap wire in the lower groove apply tinsel up the right hand spiral groove and finish by wrapping the wire in the top wire groove. This last process is exactly the same as used for decorating the fairing bobbin.

4. Tinsel and Wire.

This bobbin requires a little more skill.

- Cut a piece of tinsel about 6mm ($^1/_4$ inch) shorter than the length of the area to be covered and about 15mm ($^5/_8$ inch) wide.

- Glue one edge centrally to the middle section of the bobbin. *(Fig. 42.8).*

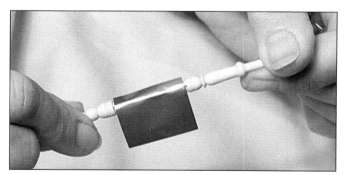

Fig. 42.8. Gluing the tinsel.

- Take the wire, bend the end, and thread it in the drilled hole at the tail end of the decoration area.

- Twist the bobbin anti-clockwise and wrap a band of wire at the end.

- Trap the first part of the tinsel taking care not to crumple it.

- Wrap the tinsel around the centre part of the bobbin.

- Now carefully wrap the tinsel with an even, loose spiral of wire until it is close to the top end. *(Fig. 42.9).*

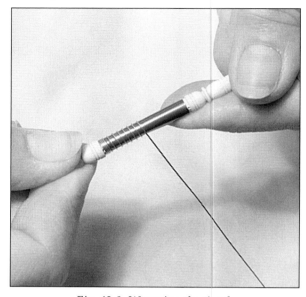

Fig. 42.9. Wrapping the tinsel.

- Finally wind a band of wire at the top to complete the bobbin. Finish off by threading wire through the drilled hole at the top of the decoration area then pull the wire tightly through using pliers. Clip off the excess wire close to the bobbin.

5. Bead Decoration.

- If you have, or are fortunate enough to have, a selection of very fine beads then the 30 gauge wire may be needed.

- Judge the number of beads required to fill the decoration area then thread that number, plus thirty, onto the wire.

- Begin the wrapping as you would any other wire decoration rotating the bobbin anti-clockwise.

- Wrap a 6mm ($^1/_4$ inch) wide area at the base of the decoration area then bring the first bead forward.

- Allow it to drop into the first groove but maintain the tension on the wire.

- Continue winding the wire, do not drop a bead into the next groove but drop into the following.

- So, bead in a groove, miss a groove, bead in a groove, miss a groove, continue in this way the length of the bobbin until within 6mm ($^1/_4$ inch) of the top of the decoration area. *(Fig. 42.10).*

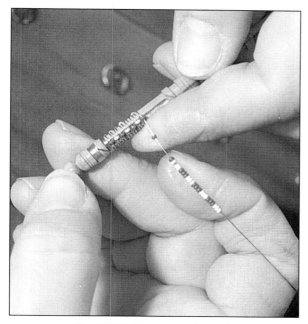

Fig. 42.10. Dropping a bead off.

- Remember to maintain tension on the wire throughout.

- Push the remaining beads, up the wire, out of the way and wrap the last section with wire as described earlier.

- Once the principle of bead wrapping is understood then the arrangement of beads on the wire can be worked so that the desired pattern can be achieved. If a coloured bead falls in the wrong place, upsetting the pattern, it is far easier to break it off with pliers and continue winding than taking any other course of action.

6. Chevron Beaded.

To demonstrate how beads will "fall" when decorating a chevron beaded bobbin we will imagine that only black and white beads are available for use.

- Thread onto 30 gauge brass wire alternate black and white beads.

- Start as before with a small bend in the end of the wire. This is anchored in the drilled hole at the start of the decoration area.

- Begin turning the bobbin anti-clockwise, with the wire under tension, and wrap an area of wire about 3mm ($^1/_8$ inch) wide.

- When the first groove is reached drop off a bead.

- Continue to drop beads off in each groove and this will produce white diagonals one way and black diagonals the other. *(Fig. 42.11).*

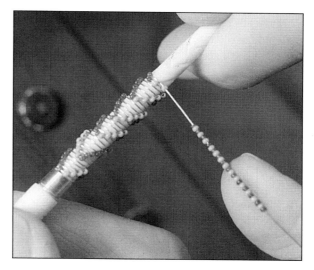

Fig. 42.11. Bead into the groove.

- Maintain tension whilst winding the wire and continue to drop off beads in all the grooves until all the chevrons have been filled.

- A point will arrive where, because of the layout of the grooves, two beads of the same colour will be needed one after the other to maintain the chevron colour pattern. Use the pliers to break off the bead which causes the problem then continue winding until the decoration is complete.

- Finish the wire wrapping at the top as described earlier to complete.

7. Gold Foil On The Loose Rings.

- From a piece of gold, paper backed, wrapping paper cut a series of 2mm ($^{1}/_{12}$ inch) wide strips.

- Apply a small amount of glue to one area on the first loose ring.

- Push one end of the strip onto the glue and press down. (*Fig. 42.12*).

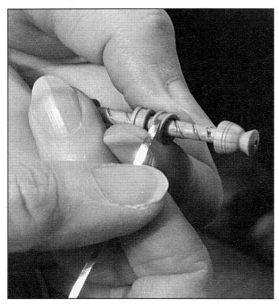

Fig. 42.12. Gluing the gold foil.

- Carefully turn the loose ring with the thumb maintaining light tension on the strip of foil.

- Continue winding the foil around the loose ring until it meets with the start.

- Cut the foil strip so that it will overlap the glued down end. (*Fig. 42.13*).

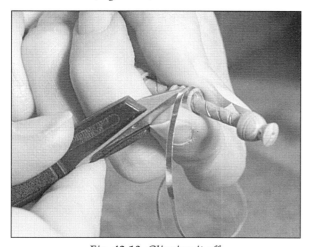

Fig. 42.13. Clipping it off.

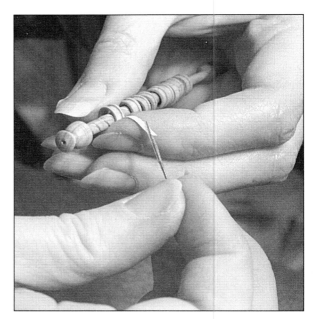

Fig. 42.14. Gluing the foil.

- Using a pin apply a small amount of glue to the back of the cut end of the foil strip. (*Fig. 42.14*).

- Press the piece down firmly making a good clean joint. (*Fig. 42.15*).

- Apply gold foil to each of the other loose rings in the same way then cover the mock loose rings at the top using the same method.

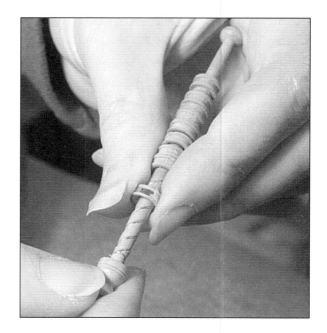

Fig. 42.15. The finished ring.

Useful Addresses

Ashley Illes Ltd.
East Kirby, Spilsby
Lincs, PE23 4DD
 — For 6mm ($^1/_4$ inch) tool steel and a variety of excellent turning tools.

Any B & Q Store
 — Brass Manifold plugs.

Craft Supplies Ltd.
228 The Mill
Miller Dale, Nr Buxton
Derbyshire, SK17 8SN
 — Crushed Velvet Blanks
 — Dymondwood Blanks

J Crispin & Sons
92-96 Curtam Rd.
London, EC2A 3AA
 — Inlay, Veneer

Halesowen Horn Co. Ltd.
PO Box 5
136 Stourbridge Rd.
Halesowen, B63 3UW
 — Horn

Stuart Johnson
The Stables Workshop
The Holloway, Market Place
Warwick, CV14 4SJ
 — Bone Pieces

Le Ronka
84 Vyse St. Hockley
Birmingham, B18 6HA
 — Pendant Drill and Burs

Spangles
Carole Morris
1, Casburn Lane, Burwell
Cambridgeshire, CB5 0ED
 — Wire and Beads

Museums that have displays of old lace bobbins.

Luton Museum & Art Gallery
Wardown Park
Luton
LU2 7HA

Bedford Museum
Castle Close
Bedford
MK40 3NY

Aylesbury Museum
Aylesbury
Buckinghamshire